The Art of Styling Sentences

20 Patterns for Success

Second Edition

by

Marie L. Waddell
Late, The University of Texas at El Paso

Robert M. Esch
Associate Professor

Roberta R. Walker
Associate Professor Emerita

Department of English
The University of Texas at El Paso

Barron's Educational Series, Inc.
Woodbury, New York • London • Toronto • Sydney

All inquiries should be addressed to:

Barron's Educational Series, Inc.
113 Crossways Park Drive
Woodbury, New York 11797

Library of Congress Catalog Card No. 81-19102

International Standard Book No. 0-8120-2269-6

Library of Congress Cataloging in Publication Data

Waddell, Marie L.
The art of styling sentences.

1. English language—Sentences. 2. English language—Rhetoric. I. Esch, Robert M. II. Walker, Roberta R. III. Title.
PE1441.W25 1983 808′.042 81-19102
ISBN 0-8120-2269-6 (pbk.)

PRINTED IN THE UNITED STATES OF AMERICA

56 800 9876543

Preface

The idea behind the twenty patterns—that students can learn to write by imitating patterns—grew out of our classroom experiences after we discovered that teaching by rules almost never will work, but that teaching by patterns nearly always will. Actually, this approach is not a new one. The teaching of writing by the imitation of patterns goes back to the pedagogy of the Renaissance; it was a common practice in the schools of Elizabethan England; it was certainly a widespread method of teaching in America from colonial times until early in the twentieth century. Our literary history shows that most great stylists of English—Shakespeare, Bacon, Donne, Milton, Jefferson, Churchill—learned to create good sentences by imitating examples from earlier literary masters. Current novelists, popular essayists, and scholars in all fields, using as they do sentence patterns like the ones in CHAPTER 2 of this book, also reflect in their writing their debt to the past, to the early masters of English prose.

The validity of teaching by imitation, by patterns for sentence structure and punctuation, became evident as we watched our students improve their ability to write, once they had sentences to imitate. Like Topsy, this book "just growed." It grew with help from colleagues in our department; our students helped us learn just what patterns they needed most often to get style and variety in their writing; other teachers offered encouragement and helpful suggestions as our patterns increased from ten to the basic twenty. The book evolved still further as we presented these twenty patterns in an English journal, in a statewide meeting of college teachers, in numerous workshops, seminars, and classes for graduate teaching assistants planning to teach English composition.

To our students who have mastered these patterns, who have made suggestions now reflected in the explanation sections, and who have contributed many of the examples, we are deeply grateful. We are deeply indebted to Dr. W. R. Lacey, Mrs. Piney Kiska, and Mrs. Marjorie Thurston, who made valuable suggestions about the manuscript. We are also grateful to our other associates on this campus and elsewhere; their encouragement and support for this technique has helped us prove once again that the Renaissance tradition of teaching by imitation will work better than teaching by rules alone. We hope that this book will provide another link in that tradition.

Marie L. Waddell
Robert M. Esch
Roberta R. Walker

THE UNIVERSITY OF TEXAS
AT EL PASO
FEBRUARY 1, 1972

Preface to the Second Edition

In preparing this revision, we have had to work without the assistance of our late co-author and colleague, Marie Waddell. We have missed her guiding hand and perceptive observations.

In revising, we have tried to eliminate dreary sentences with dated or dull topics. We have also tried to provide both teacher and student with new techniques on sentence combining and the cumulative sentence. The exercises should challenge students to work with each pattern. We appreciate the many responses we've had from those of you who have used this text successfully for the past decade. We particularly want to thank Gene Collins of the El Paso Community College and Hazel Hanley of the University of Minnesota for their detailed comments and suggestions for revisions. We invite further responses to this revision.

Roberta R. Walker
Robert M. Esch

THE UNIVERSITY OF TEXAS
AT EL PASO
SEPTEMBER 1, 1983

Contents

INTRODUCTION

Almost anyone can benefit by learning more about writing sentences. You don't have to be a student to benefit from this book; all you need is the desire to write well. And you must certainly want to create better sentences or you would not be reading this page. If you know how to write good, basic sentences yet find that they still lack something, that they sound immature because they have no variety, no style, then this little book is for you.

But if you want to write better sentences, how do you go about doing it? It's simple. You learn to write better sentences just the way you learn almost every other skill: by imitating the examples of those who already have that skill. You probably have already discovered that it is easier to master anything—whether it is jumping hurdles, doing a swan dive, or playing the guitar—if you are willing to practice imitating a model. Nowhere is this principle more obvious than in writing. If you are willing to improve your writing skills by copying models of clear sentences, then the following five chapters will help you to master the skill of writing well, gracefully, and with style.

The whole is the sum of its parts

CHAPTER 1 reviews briefly what constitutes a sentence. If you don't understand the functions of different parts of a sentence, you may need a supplementary book with a fuller discussion of sentence structure. This chapter briefly reviews the various parts of the sentence utilizing the traditional terms you will find in the explanations of the patterns in CHAPTER 2. Analyze these sentences until you understand their various parts.

Skill comes from practice

CHAPTER 2, the heart of this book, contains twenty different sentence patterns, some with variations. Study the graphic picture of each pattern (the material in the numbered boxes) and notice the precise punctuation demanded for that pattern; you will then be able to imitate these different kinds of sentences. The explanations under each boxed pattern will further clarify HOW and WHEN you should use a particular pattern; the examples will give you models to imitate; the exercises will give you practice. With these as guides, try writing and revising until you master the skill of constructing better sentences.

As you revise, take some of your original sentences and rewrite them to fit some of these patterns. This technique may at first seem too deliberate, too contrived an attempt at an artificial style. Some of the sentences you create may not seem natural. But what may seem like mere artifice at first will ultimately be the means to greater ease in writing with flair and style.

Clear writing comes from rewriting

Your first draft of any communication—letter, theme, report, written or oral speech—will almost always need revision. When you first try to express ideas, you are mainly interested in capturing your elusive thoughts, in making them concrete enough on a sheet of paper for you to think about them. The second step in the writing process—in fact, where writing really begins—is revision, an on-going process. You must work deliberately to express your captured ideas in clear and graceful sentences.

Combinations lead to endless variety

CHAPTER 3 will show you how some of the basic twenty styling patterns in CHAPTER 2 can combine with other patterns. Study the examples given and described in CHAPTER 3; then let your imagination direct your own efforts at making effective combinations of the different patterns.

Imagination is one cornerstone of style

CHAPTER 4 will show you how to express your thoughts in imaginative, figurative language. Study the pattern for each figure of speech described there, and then deliberately try to insert an occasional one—simile, metaphor, analogy, or allusion—into your own writing. Or you might experiment with an ironical tone. Try to be original; never merely echo some well-known, ready-made cliché. Create new images from your own experiences, from your own way of looking at life.

Understanding comes from analysis

CHAPTER 5 contains excerpts from the works of experienced writers who have incorporated patterns like these in their paragraphs. Study the marginal notes which give the pattern numbers you have learned from studying CHAPTER 2. Then analyze something you are reading; discover for yourself how writers handle their sentences and their punctuation. Don't be afraid to imitate them when you write. You will, of course, find "patterns" (arrangements of words in sentences) that are not in CHAPTER 2 of this book. Imitate others as well as the twenty we present.

SUGGESTIONS FOR THE INSTRUCTOR

Since this method of teaching students to write by imitation will be new to some instructors, we hope this section will offer helpful and practical suggestions. For the new teacher we want to anticipate some possible questions and provide some classroom guidelines; for the experienced teacher, we hope to offer a fresh approach to an old problem: getting students to write papers that are not too dull and boring for them to write or for us to read. The following pages contain some hints for ways of teaching material in CHAPTERS 1 and 2. Additional pages addressed to students also suggest valuable ways for the teacher to present the patterns and other techniques to a class. For further justification of teaching by imitating rhetorical models, see Richard L. Graves, "Levels of Skill in the Composing Process," *CCC,* 29 (October, 1978), 231–32, and Rosemary Hake and Joseph M. Williams, "Sentence Expanding: Not Can, or How, But When," *Sentence Combining and the Teaching of Writing* (L&S Books, University of Akron, 1979).

Sentence Combining

Concurrent with publication of the first edition of *The Art of Styling Sentences,* a number of researchers developed a teaching technique that is quite different from the "imitation" method described in this book. The technique of sentence combining, introduced first by John Mellon in *Transformational Sentence Combining* (NCTE, 1969), and later developed in Frank O'Hare's NCTE study, *Sentence Combining,* Research Report #15 (1971) and *Sentencecraft* (Ginn, 1975), in William Strong's *Sentence Combining* (Random House, 1973, 1983) and *Sentence Combining and Paragraph Linking* (Random House, 1979), and in Donald Daiker, *et al., The Writer's Options* (Harper, 1979), refers to a practice of deriving from a variety of sentences, usually short, simple, kernel sentences, a pattern for combining them into one or two longer sentences. Other texts soon followed, providing additional practice for students using this technique: Michelle Rippon and Walter E. Meyers, *Combining Sentences* (Harcourt, 1979) and Katie Davis, *Sentence Combining and Paragraph Construction* (Macmillan, 1983). Through this type of practice the student develops syntactic maturity. The result of this method is effective skill building; the students' sentences have greater variety, appear more mature and sophisticated, and illustrate how writers in the same class, working with the same kernel sentences, are able to transform them into many different types of effective communication.

Here is a sample list of ten kernels that students might transform:

1. The guard dribbled the ball down the court.
2. The guard was a muscular man.
3. The guard was about 6′4″.
4. The center was down court.
5. The center waved his hands.
6. The center yelled for the ball and motioned to the guard.
7. The center called out a number for a play.
8. An opposing guard ran in front of the center.
9. He was 6′8″ tall.
10. He had arms like a giant.
11. The center reached high into the air.
12. He grabbed the pass out of the air.
13. He swiveled and leaped up to dunk the ball.
14. The team won by two points.

Suggestions for teaching chapter 1

As we said in the introduction to the book, CHAPTER 1, "The Sentence," does not pretend to be a complete discussion of sentence structure. The English sentence took several centuries to develop and is, as Sir Winston Churchill said, a "noble thing" indeed. There are entire books dedicated to an explanation of it; hence our coverage is minimal.

The main thing to do with CHAPTER 1 is to review with your class the five important "slots" in the standard sentence—subject, verb, complement, modifier, and connector. Be sure the students understand the terms and the functions of each. Give them some class practice in separating subjects from verbs in any of their current reading. It is sometimes easier for them to find the essential skeleton of the sentence if first they cross out, or put in parentheses, all of the prepositional phrases (which are usually modifiers, anyway). Then let them discuss the differences between phrases and clauses, between independent and dependent structures, between declarative and imperative sentences. Never assume that students will be very adept at this kind of analysis. Therefore guide them carefully with detailed explanation and many examples on the board or on transparencies you might prepare.

Suggestions for teaching chapter 2—the patterns

CHAPTER 2, "The Twenty Patterns," is the heart of this book and contains enough material to keep your students busy throughout the semester as they incorporate the material into their compositions. Pace your discussions to fit your class; don't go faster than your class can master the techniques, and never try to cover more than three patterns in any one class period. You will find that there is a logical grouping and arrangement of the patterns, so you might find it easier to go straight through from PATTERN 1 to PATTERN 20.

You will need to explain each of these patterns in great detail; you will also need to justify the rationale of the punctuation. Before you start with PATTERN 1, put some sentences on the board and review the sentence structure from CHAPTER 1. A good place to begin any kind of analysis of sentences is to have students put parentheses around all prepositional phrases, using anything from their current reading—a textbook, the sports page, an advertisement, lyrics of a popular song, or the label on a ketchup bottle or a beer can! This is an effective exercise because prepositional phrases are nearly always modifiers of something and almost never a part of the basic sentence.

Now, with your class, create appropriate graphic symbols to use when you analyze and discuss sentences. You can use a double bar (||) to separate independent clauses or brackets to set off dependent clauses, something like the following:

1. Draw one line under the main clause (in this case, the entire sentence):

   The atom bomb || exploded our old world and mushroomed us into a new age.

2. Dramatize what happens when there are two independent clauses in the same sentence:

The atom bomb || shattered our old world (into smithereens;) it || suddenly mushroomed us (into a completely new kind) (of world).

Draw a circle between the two independent clauses (which *could* be separate sentences); then explain that only four things can occur:

a. the period—which would separate these into two sentences;

b. a coordinating conjunction *(and, or, but, nor, for, so, yet)* preceded by a comma;

c. a semicolon—sometimes with a connective like *therefore* or *however;*

d. a colon—but *only if* the second sentence explains or extends the idea of the first.

3. Use a bracket to set off dependent clauses and clarify their function as PART of the independent clause:

Marcie || bought [whatever she | wanted.]
[What Tatum | needs] || is more discipline.
The little children || played [where the fallen leaves | were deep and soft.]

4. Use a wavy line under an absolute phrase:

The war being over at last, the task (of arranging the peace terms) || began.

5. Use a circle around connectors and other non-functional terms.

Next, it might be fun to show that these constructions work even with nonsense words. Do one or two and then let the class put their own creations on the board and explain them.

A bronsly sartian || swazzled (along the tentive clath.)
Yesterday I || thrombled (down the nat-fleuzed beach) [where glorphs and mizzles | lay (in the sun).]

After this review, the class should be ready to tackle the first group of sentence patterns—the compounds. All of them are really just two sentences in one, but with a vast difference that you must make clear. Now is the time to have the class really master the Checkpoints under PATTERN 3, which cover the differences in the three compounds.

For exercises beyond those that accompany the pattern explanations, consider these ideas:

1. Follow your discussion of particular patterns by asking students to write ten sentences of their own using the patterns you assign. Have students label each sentence with the number of the pattern in the **left** margin. *The advantage of this book is the control you have through the pattern numbers.* For subject matter students can draw upon their reading, hobbies, sports, and other interests. If for any given assignment the entire class uses the same topic or idea, have the students compare how many different arrangements of words can express the same idea but with slightly different emphasis or rhythm.
2. Use SENTENCE PATTERN **1**, the compound with a semicolon and without a conjunction, to teach or to test vocabulary. In the first clause of the compound have students USE and UNDERSCORE the word in a sentence; in the second part have them DEFINE that word in a sentence.

   EXAMPLE: Zen Buddhism is an *esoteric* philosophy; only the initiated really understand it.

   OR THIS VARIATION:

   The Greek root chrono means "time"; a chronometer measures time accurately. (See how much you can teach about punctuation in a sentence with this structure!)
3. Assign ten vocabulary words, each to be written in a different sentence pattern. Have students underscore the vocabulary word and label the pattern by number in the left margin. If students give the pattern number of the structure they are imitating, you can check the accuracy of their understanding of the pattern at the same time you are checking the vocabulary word.
4. Require students to have at least one different pattern in each paragraph of their compositions. Have them label each sentence

by writing in the left margin the number of the pattern they are imitating. See "Marginalia: to encourage deliberate craftsmanship" (pp. xviii–xxii) for more ways to encourage students in analyzing their writing as they improve their craftsmanship.

5. Have students collect interesting sentences from their reading and make a booklet of fifteen or twenty new and different patterns with no more than two or three sentences plus analysis on each page. They may simply copy the sentences they find or they may clip and paste them to the booklet pages, leaving room for a description (analysis) of each sentence in their own words.
6. Take a long, involved sentence from the assigned reading; have your students rewrite it several times using four or five different sentence patterns. (These revisions may have to contain some words that the original does not have.) Have students read these sentences aloud in class, commenting on the various effects thus achieved.
7. Point out the effectiveness of incorporating PATTERN 8 (the one with two or three dependent clauses) in a thesis or using it to forecast main points in the introduction or to summarize in the conclusion.
8. Toward the end of the term, after they have mastered the patterns and know them by number, have students analyze some of their current reading, even from other courses. Have them write in the margin the numbers of the sentence patterns they find. (See CHAPTER 5 for two examples of this.)

SUGGESTIONS FOR THE STUDENT

How to get the most from this book

The suggestions and exercises below may seem too simple or too artificial at first sight, but if you make a game of playing around with words, of fitting them to the formula, you will probably enjoy yourself. You will certainly learn how to write sentences that have some flair, and that is a skill worth developing because a well-constructed sentence is, like any artful design, the result of good craftsmanship; it actually involves and requires:

1. good composing or construction
2. accurate punctuation
3. a feeling for the rhythm of language
4. an understanding of idiom
5. clarity of expression

If you are not in a composition class, but are working alone without a teacher's guidance, the suggestions below will help you to get the most out of this book, so do follow them carefully. Don't be afraid to copy a pattern and fit your own words into it. Remember that all great craftsmen begin as apprentices imitating a master. By following the suggestions below and mastering the sentence patterns, you will increase your skill in the art of styling sentences.

1. Study one pattern at a time. Write four or five sentences that follow that pattern exactly, especially the punctuation. Go through all twenty patterns in CHAPTER 2, taking only one at a time, until you are confident you understand the structure and the punctuation. Practice, practice—and more practice: this is the only way to learn.

2. In every paragraph you write, try to incorporate one or more of these patterns, especially when you find yourself tending to write "primer sentences," those short and simple sentences having the same kind of subject—verb structure. Deliberately keep trying to improve the quality and arrangement of all of your sentences, whether they follow one of these patterns or not.

3. Think of something you want to say and then practice writing it in three or four different ways, noticing the changes in effect and tone when you express the same idea with different patterns and punctuation. You may not be aware of these changes unless you read aloud, so do it often because reading out loud will train your ear.

4. Analyze your reading material for interesting sentences, ones that you think have striking patterns you could imitate. (CHAPTER 5 shows you how.) Whether you are reading a newspaper, a magazine article, or a skillfully styled literary work, you will find many sentences so well written that you will want to analyze and then imitate. Underline them; learn the pattern. Or from your reading make a collection of sentences that you have especially enjoyed. Or keep a special notebook of new and different patterns that you want to copy. In short, look for new and different kinds of sentences in everything you read and make a conscious effort to add those new patterns to the basic twenty in CHAPTER 2.

Marginalia: to encourage deliberate craftsmanship

Analysis for themes

In every theme or paper you write there should be some goals, some design that you are trying to fulfill. Marginalia can be a helpful guide for you, a way of checking up on what you are doing when you write. Marginalia is simply an analysis, which you write in the left margin; it consists of words and symbols that indicate your analysis of what you do when you write.

In the first themes of the semester your teacher will probably be highly prescriptive, more than later on. When you are told how many words, how many paragraphs, sometimes even how many sentences should occur within paragraphs, don't resent the detailed directions. Think about them as training in a skill. After all, athletic coaches and music teachers alike begin their training with strict regulations and drills, too. So follow all the "requirements." Eventually, they will become a part of your skill as a writer, something you do instinctively. Then, you can dispense with marginalia.

Things to do

1. Highlight the topic sentence of each paragraph. Identify by the label **TS** in the margin.
2. In the **left** margin of each paragraph, indicate the attempted pattern from the SENTENCE PATTERNS (**SP**). Mark in the margin **SP 6** or **SP 9a**, for example.
3. Indicate a pronoun reference pattern in one of the paragraphs by drawing a circle around the pronouns and an arrow pointing to their antecedent. Identify in margin as **PRO PATT.**
4. Circle transitional words in one paragraph ("echo" words, transitional connectives, conjunctions).
5. List in the margin the types of sentences in one paragraph; be sure that there are simple (**S**), complex (**CX**), compound (**C**), and compound complex (**CCX**) sentences—at least one of each type.
6. When you master a new vocabulary word, underline it and label it **VOC.**

You might use a different color for each type of entry so that you can see at a glance that you have incorporated all the techniques of good construction. These marks might seem distracting at first, but the results will be worth the distraction. A glance at the marginalia will indicate whether you understand the composition techniques being taught.

Why bother with all of this? Because it works. There is no better answer. You will come to realize that themes must have a variety of sentences, that there must be transitional terms if the theme is to have coherence, that pronouns help eliminate needless repetition of the same word, that synonyms and figurative language give the theme more sparkle than you ever hoped for. Your teachers will like what they are reading; you will like what you are writing, and your grades will improve.

The following pages show two paragraphs written by a student. Note the marginal analysis and the effectiveness of the different sentence patterns.

A paragraph analyzing a simile in poetry

The Movement of Time

"Like as the waves make towards the pebbled shore,
So do our minutes hasten to their end . . . ."

—*William Shakespeare,* SONNET LX

In the first two lines of Sonnet LX, Shakespeare uses a simile comparing the waves of the ocean to the minutes of our life: "Like as the waves make towards the pebbled shore, / So do our minutes hasten to their end . . . ." This line is inverted: that is, the subject "our minutes" is in the second line, and the comparison "like as the waves" is in the first line. The simile says, in effect, that "the minutes of our lives are like the waves on the shore." The waves roll endlessly, inexorably toward the shore of the ocean; the minutes of our lives hasten endlessly toward the end of our lives. This figure of speech gives an image of movement. We can almost see time, like ocean waves, moving toward its destiny: the end of life. Just as the waves end on the shore, so too our life's minutes end in death. Some words in the simile have particular power: the word *hasten* conjures up a mental picture of rapid movement, of inexorable hurry toward some predestined end. The word *towards* suggests a straight, unerring path going without hesitation or pause to some goal. The waves move toward their goal: the shore. Our minutes move toward their goal: life's end. This simile is a very effective, picture-making figure of speech. It paints a mental picture of movement and destiny. It suggests a very important fact about life, a fact we must remember. That fact is the truth expressed here beautifully by Shakespeare—life goes on forever toward its end, never slowing down or going back. Our lives do indeed "hasten to their end."

—Shawn Waddell

MARGINALIA

TS

SP3
SP11

VOC
SP1

SP10
SP16
SP3
VOC
a repeated SVO pattern

repeated SP10

PRO PATT
SP9
Repeat of keyword

Summary of TS with "echo" of quote

A paragraph defining a term

A Junk-man

MARGINALIA

TS
Order: General to Particular
SP4A
SP14
SP12
VOC
Metaphor
VOC
SP1
SP10
and 4a
Contrast
SP9
Definition of TS
repeated word for coherence
Example
factual data
Contrast
VOC and two levels of diction

A junk-man in baseball is the most feared pitcher of all. Most batters go to the plate with the knowledge that the pitcher usually throws either curves or fastballs or knuckleballs in the clinch. From his view at the plate, a batter sees a curveballpitcher's curve starting off in a line seemingly headed straight for his head. Fortunately, just before making any painful contact, the ball seems to change its own mind, veering away to the opposite side of the plate. But after long and arduous practice, any batter can learn to anticipate or recognize a curve and be prepared for it. The same is true for a fastball that blurs its way into the catcher's mitt or for a knuckleball which seems to have trouble deciding where to go. A veteran batter can learn to sense the sometimes erratic path of either ball; he can feel some confidence when he has some idea of the pitcher's preferred ball: a curve or a fastball or a knuckleball; he can even learn to make that wonderful contact which means a hit. But he can be put completely off stride when he hears he has to face that most dreaded of all pitchers, a junk-man—dreaded because he can throw all pitches with equal effectiveness and surprise. This element of surprise coupled with variety makes the junk-man the most feared of all pitchers in baseball. For example, when Sam the Slugger goes to bat, he can feel more relaxed if he knows that Carl the Curve-man will probably throw curves about seventy-five percent of the time; Sam can then, more than likely, be ready for at least one—which incidentally is all he needs to be ready for. The same is true for Sam when a well-known fastballer or knuckler is facing him from sixty feet away. On the contrary Sam the Slugger loses his equanimity and is tied in knots when Joe the Junk-man grins wickedly across that

SP1

echo of TS for coherence

short sixty feet from mound to plate; Sam has no way to anticipate what surprises may lurk behind that wicked grin when he faces the most feared pitcher in baseball.

—Shawn Waddell

CHAPTER 1

THE SENTENCE

What exactly is a sentence?

Like sign language, the beat of drums, or smoke signals, sentences are a means of communicating. They may express emotion, give orders, make statements, or ask questions; but in every case they try to communicate.

In most sentences there are two parts which follow a basic pattern:

Subject || Verb

Occasionally, a sentence may be a single word:

What? Nonsense! Exaggerate.

In certain contexts "What?" and "Nonsense!" may communicate a complete thought. "Exaggerate," as you can see, has an implied "you" as its subject.

Now let's break up a very simple type of sentence into its two parts.

The bees are swarming.
The zebras stampeded.

bees	||	are swarming

Try making up your own example following the pattern above; box the subject and verb, and insert a pair of vertical lines between these two basic parts of the sentence. Only two slots are necessary—the S (subject) slot and the V (verb) slot.

Now let's add modifiers to the subject, to the verb, or to both. Note that you still have but two slots and need only one pair of vertical lines:

The agitated bees	||	are swarming in the apricot trees.
The startled zebras	||	stampeded the white hunters.

Combining the S slot and the V slot, you can construct the most common sentence pattern. Each one has a traditional name, describing its purpose and the task it performs:

TASK	NAME
A sentence may make a statement.	Declarative
May it also ask a question?	Interrogative
Give an order.	Imperative
What great emotion it can express!	Exclamatory

As you add words to modify the subject and verb, you will create longer sentences, some with phrases, others with clauses. Quite simply, a *phrase* is a group of words containing no subject—verb combination but acting as a modifier. A *clause* is a group of words containing a subject—verb combination; sometimes the clause expresses a complete thought, but not always.

INDEPENDENT CLAUSE	makes a complete statement communicates an idea by itself
DEPENDENT CLAUSE	modifies a unit in another clause does not communicate a complete thought may be a unit in another clause.

These two types of clauses combine to form various types of sentences, but the most common sentences are these:

SIMPLE	makes a single statement is an independent clause has a subject—verb combination
COMPOUND	makes two or more statements has two or more independent clauses has two or more subject—verb combina tions
COMPLEX	has an independent clause has one or more dependent clauses functioning as modifiers
COMPOUND COMPLEX	has two or more independent clauses has two or more subject—verb combinations has one or more dependent clauses functioning as modifiers

The subject—verb combination is the heart of each sentence you write. With this combination you can build an infinite variety of more intricate sentence patterns. Each new subject—verb combination will require a new pair of || lines. Longer sentences may have only one S and one V slot with one pair of vertical lines. Sometimes there will be only *one* subject in the S slot; sometimes there will be *two or more* subjects, all in the same S slot, because they come before the vertical lines separating S from V. The verb slot also may have one verb or several verbs.

Elizabeth and Mary Tudor || were sisters but hated each other.

Sentences often have an added attraction—something after the verb which is neither a modifying word nor a phrase—yet even these sentences may have but one S and one V slot. If the verb is transitive, you will find a direct object following it. In the following examples (all simple sentences), direct objects appear.

EXAMPLE: Ben || forgot his galoshes.

Agnes || ignored her teacher's glares and continued her mischief-making.

NOTE: Throughout this chapter one line will underline the subject; two lines, the verb.

If the verb is intransitive, however, there may be subject completers (subject complements) which are nouns, pronouns, or adjectives. The following sentences illustrate the single S—V combination with one or more subject complements.

EXAMPLE: Anne Boleyn was Henry VIII's second wife.

Bargain basement sales may be ________ or ________, ________ or ________, ________ or ________.

(YOU *try filling in the blanks above!)*

To almost every part of the sentence you may add modifying words and phrases. You will still retain the single subject—verb combination or else expand your sentence to include several subject—verb combinations, all having modifiers. Distinguish main clauses by putting || between the S and the V in the main clause and | between the S and the

V in the dependent clauses; then underline independent clauses and put brackets around dependent clauses.

EXAMPLE: Long or short sentences || can sometimes communicate effectively the most difficult ideas in the world. (simple)

Sterling silver [that || may cost $800 a place setting] and small kitchen appliances like can openers or toasters [that || are considered too basic] are no longer popular wedding gifts. (complex)

Now let's break the whole sentence into its parts. When making a mechanical analysis of any sentence, you should use the following labels to identify the various parts:

S subject
V verb
C connective (conjunction)
O object of preposition; object of infinitive
M modifier
IO indirect object
SC subject complement
P preposition
DO direct object

The following sentence illustrates the type of analysis you might practice:

M The **M** rundown, **M** dirty **S** shoes **V** appeared **M** unbelievably **SC** incongruous **P** on **M** the **O** model.

The following chapters in this manual will help you to write more effective sentences and will give you clues to spice up dreary prose. Sentences come to life as a writer plans them; in fact, very few fine sentences are spontaneous. The following pages have models for sentences that you may imitate and use. The patterns presented are basic, but by no means are they the only ones. As your writing matures, you will discover additional patterns. As you master the ability to analyze and to compose sentences, you will justifiably be proud of your improving style.

And now you're off . . . on the way to creating better sentences, more polished paragraphs.

For detailed information, materials, and examples of the sentence, you might wish to consult a recently edited handbook or one of the following rhetorics:

Hartwell, Patrick. *Open to Language.* New York: Oxford University Press, Inc., 1982. (see esp. Unit III, pp. 167–292)

Hefferman, James and John Lincoln. *Writing: A College Handbook.* New York: W.W. Norton & Co., Inc., 1982. (see esp. pp. 201–418)

Jacobus, Lee. *The Sentence Book.* New York: Harcourt Brace, 1976.

Students in advanced composition courses should also consult the discussions of sentences in these texts:

Coe, Richard. *Form and Substance.* New York: John Wiley & Sons, Inc., 1981. (see esp. pp. 182ff)

Corbett, Edward. *Classical Rhetoric for the Modern Student,* 2nd ed. Chicago: University of Chicago Press, 1977.

Hairston, Maxine. *Successful Writing.* New York: W.W. Norton & Co., Inc., 1981. (see esp. Chapter 7)

Hirsch, E. D. *The Philosophy of Composition.* Chicago: University of Chicago Press, 1977.

Lanham, Richard. *Revising Prose.* New York: Scribners, 1979.

CHAPTER 2

THE TWENTY PATTERNS

Now let's make sentences grow . . .

This chapter introduces you to twenty basic patterns, which writers frequently use to help give their style flavor and variety. These will not be new to you; you've already seen them many times in things you've read. Perhaps you have never thought about analyzing them, nor realized they could help you perk up your prose. But they can.

Study them—give them a chance to help you.

Compound constructions

In the first chapter you studied the most elementary kinds of sentences. The easiest way to expand this basic pattern is simply to join two short complete statements (simple sentences) and thereby make a compound. When you do this, be sure to avoid two pitfalls of the compound sentence:

1. the fused or run-on sentence (which has no punctuation between the two sentences that have been joined);
2. the comma splice (which is a mere comma instead of a period, semicolon, or colon to separate the two sentences you have now joined).

A comma between independent clauses must have *and, but, or, yet, so, nor,* or *for* with it. Of course, you will have no trouble avoiding these two pitfalls if you faithfully copy the following patterns for compound sentences, being careful to imitate punctuation exactly, too.

PATTERN 1:	COMPOUND SENTENCE: SEMICOLON, NO CONJUNCTION (two short, related sentences now joined)
	S V ; S V .

EXPLANATION:

This pattern helps you join two short, simple sentences having two closely related ideas. Simply let a semicolon take the place of a conjunction with a comma. The graphic illustration in the box above and the examples below show only two clauses; you may, of course, have three or more.

And remember what makes a complete clause: a subject–verb combination that makes a full statement. In other words, an independent, complete clause must have a finite verb; therefore look for one on each side of the semicolon. Remember that what precedes and what follows the semicolon in a compound sentence (PATTERN 1) must be capable of standing alone as a sentence.

This is a fragment:

> The reason for the loss in yardage being
> the broken shoe-string on the left guard's shoe.

"Being" is the wrong verb form; change it to "was" and make a sentence.

This is another kind of fragment:

> Which was the only explanation that he could give at that moment.

This fragment is a dependent clause, in spite of the subject—verb combinations (*which was* and *he could*), because of the subordinating word (in this case, a relative pronoun) at the beginning. Remember this equation:

Because If When After	+ (plus)	a subject-verb combination	= (equals)	a fragment every time.

and other such subordinating words

EXAMPLES:

Caesar, try on this toga; it seems to be your size.

"Success has many fathers; failure is an orphan."
—John F. Kennedy

The air conditioner was no longer adequate; it was time to buy a whole new system.

The vicuña is a gentle animal living in the central Andes; its fleece often becomes the fabric for expensive coats.

Some men dream of being something; others stay awake and are.

Man is related to the monkey; only a monkey, however, would ever admit the relationship.

CHECKPOINTS:

✔ Check to see that on both sides of the semicolon there is a complete statement (sentence).

ERROR: Failure to have two independent clauses
EXAMPLE: Standing behind this very country gentleman is a kindly, silver-haired woman; carrying a platter of dinner rolls; the typical grandmother.

✔ After a semicolon there CANNOT be a construction like one of these:

. . . . ; which is the . . . .
. . . . ; the result being. . . . .
. . . . ; although he never did . . . .

These three errors can be corrected with slight revision:

. . . . ; it is the . . . .
. . . . ; the result will be . . . .
. . . . ; he never did . . . .

✔ **ALSO,** the words before a semicolon must make a complete statement. Never put a semicolon after the following construction:

For example; . . . .
Because the snow was deep and the temperature below zero; . . . .
The work having been finished by five o'clock; . . . .

✓ These three errors can be corrected thus:
For example, ...
Because the snow was deep, the temperature fell below zero.
The work was finished by five o'clock.

✓ In short, don't confuse commas and semicolons.

VARIATIONS:

The first variation, PATTERN 1a, involves the use of conjunctive adverbs (connectors) such as *however, hence, therefore, thus, then, moreover, nevertheless, likewise, consequently,* and *accordingly.* The use of a comma after the connector is optional.

S V ; however, S V .

EXAMPLES: David had worked in the steaming jungle for two years without leave; hence he was tired almost beyond endurance.

This gadget won't work; therefore there is no sense in buying it.

For the second variation, PATTERN 1b, use a coordinating conjunction (also a connector) such as *and, or, for, but, nor, yet,* or *so.*

S V ; S V , and S V .
S V , but S V ; S V .

EXAMPLES: It was snowing outside, and in the building Harold felt safe; he dreaded leaving his shelter for the long, dangerous trip home.

It was radical; it was daring, but mostly it was cheap.

Some people blamed the judge; others blamed the defendants, and still others blamed all parties to the trial of the political prisoners, which from almost any viewpoint was a disgrace to American justice.

The squirrel in our front yard is a playful sort; he mocks us from his tree, but I can entice him from his treetop home with a few crusts of bread.

Try this third variation, PATTERN 1c:

S V ; S V ; S V .

EXAMPLES: North bid one club; East passed; South bid one spade; West doubled.

"To spend too much time in studies is sloth; to use them too much for ornamentation is affectation; to make judgement wholly by their rules is the humor of a scholar." —Francis Bacon

EXERCISES:

Complete the following sentences with logically expressed independent clauses.

1. ______________________________;

the city was deserted and in flames .

2. The troops bedded down early after the dawn attack ;

______________________________.

3. The cat's tail began to switch back and forth ; __________

______________________________.

Complete the following sentences by adding appropriate conjunctive adverbs.

1. The crisis had passed ; ______________ we decided to continue with our plans to leave for Spain the following week .

2. Robert would never admit that he had made a mistake ; ______________ he had definitely made an error in his income tax return .

3. Sidney was older than Grace ; ______________ his knowledge of world affairs was greater than hers .

Combine the following short sentences into one that follows PATTERN 1b. If necessary, add, omit, or change words to improve the sentence.

GROUP ONE: The team looks sad.
Victory had escaped the hockey champs.
Victory does not always go to the deserving.

____

____

GROUP TWO: Neither Nora nor Bettie has a chance of becoming the state's gymnastic champion.
Neither wants to withdraw from the contest.
Neither wants to face the realities of failure.

____

____

____

GROUP THREE: Fettucini is a delicious pasta.
It is a favorite dish in many European countries.
It is often associated with Italy.
A man who likes fettucini is not always Italian.

____

____

____

Following PATTERN 1c, create one logically structured sentence from the following word groups, adding or omitting words.

GROUP ONE
In the end they all were buried in the ancient Protestant cemetery where Madame de Rochmont was placed by choice, but the others were buried there when their time came because they had all died in Rome.

GROUP TWO
The perennial best-seller, the Bible, topped the nonfiction list with Kenneth Taylor's 1972 version, *The Living Bible,* while the top fiction seller of the 1970's was Richard Bach's *Jonathan Livingston Seagull* with Tolkien's *The Silmarillion*—a prelude to *The Hobbit*—a close second.

As you read for class assignments or pleasure, watch for sentences that follow this pattern and add them below.

PATTERN 2:	COMPOUND SENTENCE WITH ELLIPTICAL CONSTRUCTION (comma indicates the omitted verb)

S V DO or SC ; S , DO or SC .

(omitted verb)

EXPLANATION:

This pattern is really the same as PATTERN 1, but here you will omit the verb in the second clause BECAUSE and ONLY IF it would needlessly repeat the verb of the first clause anyway. In other words, the comma says to the reader, "Here you should mentally insert the same verb you have already read in the first clause."

This construction naturally implies a need for more or less parallel wording in both clauses; the verb, of course, must be exactly the same.

For example, this is not parallel:

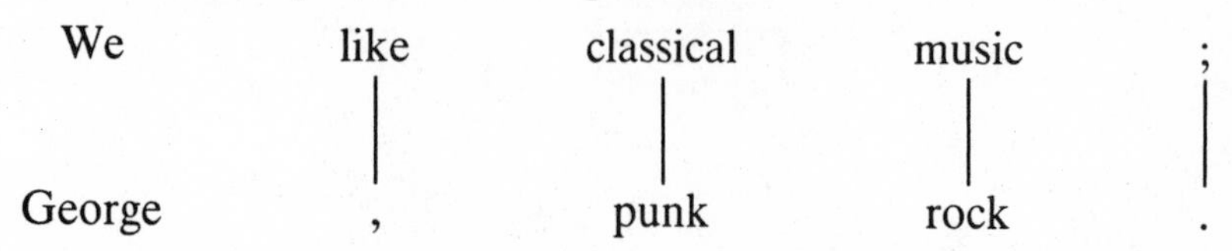

The reader could not take the verb from the first clause and put it where the comma is, because "George like punk rock" is ungrammatical and improper. BUT even if your wording is parallel, even if the omitted verb is exactly like the one in the first clause, you may still have an awkward-sounding sentence if you forget the importance of rhythm and sound.

For example, read this aloud:

Darby played a musical number by Bach; Joan, Beethoven.

This sentence, read aloud, sounds as if Darby played something written by three people!

Then read this aloud:

Darby played a musical number by Bach;
Joan, one by Beethoven.

If you leave out more than the verb, you may need to insert a word like "one" here.

Notice in the sentence above and in the two sentences below that it is possible to leave out more than just the verb; sometimes you may even leave out the subject *and* the verb:

An artist's instinct is intuitive, not rational;
aesthetic, not pragmatic.

There's an interesting difference in books on the subject of sex: in handbooks about dating, the experts tell you how to avoid it; in handbooks about marriage, how to enjoy it.

EXAMPLES:

The Christian church and communism each have a goal: one is spiritual; the other, material.

The Scottish Highlander sports a tam-o'-shanter; the Texas Ranger, a Stetson or a ten-gallon hat.

Because of the length of both oceans, the Atlantic and the Pacific share the same boundaries; the Arctic Ocean is the northern; the Antarctic, the southern.

The Russian ballerina wears a tutu; the Malaysian dancer, a brightly colored sarong.

A red light means stop; a green light, go.

"Thought is the blossom; language [,] the bud; action [,] the fruit behind it." —Ralph Waldo Emerson

CHECKPOINTS:

✔ Be sure that there really are two independent clauses here even though the second one has an unexpressed verb.

✔ Be absolutely sure that the verb omitted in the second clause matches exactly the verb in the first clause.

✔ The following rule applies to whatever you omit after the semicolon:

If you leave out more than the verb, be sure the structure is parallel and the thought is complete.

✔ Use a semicolon if there is no conjunction; use a comma if there is a joining, coordinate conjunction.

EXERCISES:

Complete the following sentences. (1) Use a comma in the second clause to substitute for the verb in the first clause. (2) Write a complete thought for a missing first clause.

1. The green light at the end of Daisy's dock represents hope for Jay ; ______________________________

 ______________________________ .

2. A threatening sky with black clouds usually signals an approaching storm ; ______________________________

 ______________________________ .

3. ______________________________ ;

 Passover and Easter, the season of renewal .

4. An owl symbolizes wisdom ; ______________________________ .

5. All the children wanted to go to McDonald's for lunch ;

 ______________________________ .

As you read for class assignments or pleasure, watch for sentences that follow this pattern and add them below.

____

____

PATTERN 3:		COMPOUND SENTENCE WITH EXPLANATORY STATEMENT (clauses separated by a colon)	
General statement (idea)	:	specific statement (example)	.
(an independent clause)		(an independent clause)	

EXPLANATION:

This pattern is exactly like PATTERNS 1 and 2 in structure: it is a compound; but it is very different in content, as the colon implies. A colon in a compound sentence performs a special function: it signals to the reader that something important or explanatory will follow (as this very sentence illustrates). In this particular pattern, the colon signals that the second clause will specifically explain or expand some idea expressed only vaguely in the first clause.

The first statement will contain a word or an idea that needs explaining; the second statement will give some specific information or example about that idea.

As you study the following examples, notice that the first independent statement mentions something in an unspecific way: "a harsh truth," "a horrifying meaning." Then the independent statement after the colon answers your questions: "What harsh truth?" "Which horrifying meaning?" In short, the second clause makes the first one clear.

EXAMPLES:

Darwin's *Origin of Species* forcibly states a harsh truth: only the fittest survive.

The empty coffin in the center of the crypt had a single horrifying meaning: Dracula had left his tomb to stalk the village streets in search of fresh blood.

Carry Amelia Nation and her female temperance league had a single goal: they hoped to smash every whiskey bottle and hatchet every saloon in America.

"Not all basketball players use the same technique in shooting free throws: some of them shoot the ball from over their heads and others use the 'granny' shot, which they shoot from the waist and project upwards." —Jimmy Salem

"Weekdays are very similar to identical suitcases: they are all the same size, but some people can pack more into them than others." —Joel Gutierrez

We have difficulty realizing that people use words in different contexts: my "cat" is not your "cat."

No one, however, would argue that George Patton did what generals were primarily expected to do: he won battles.

The politician studied the polls last week and reached a comfortable conclusion: only a disaster—or a serious mistake—could keep him from the Presidency.

A lizard never worries about losing his tail: he can always grow another.

CHECKPOINTS:

✔ Now that you have learned all three of the compound sentences, notice the differences. PATTERNS 1, 2, and 3 are NOT simply three different ways to punctuate the same sentence. The words must perform different functions; the sentences must do different things:

PATTERN 1 must make two closely related statements about the same idea, statements you do not want to punctuate as two separate sentences;

PATTERN 2 must have the exact word or words from the first clause implied in the second—otherwise no ellipsis is possible;

PATTERN 3 must have a second independent clause that in some way amplifies or explains the idea stated in the first independent clause.

✔ You should not use this pattern with a colon unless the second statement is related to the first.

✔ Remember the test for all compound sentences: both clauses must be full statements and capable of standing alone as sentences.

EXERCISES:

Complete the following sentences with independent clauses that (1) answer an implied question, (2) provide an example, or (3) give further explanation:

1. ______________________________ :

   all the graduates cheered as President Arneson conferred their degrees .

2. The products of Japan represent a genuine threat to many American industries : ______________________________

   ______________________________ .

3. At least I know one way *not* to clean out a radiator : ______

   ______________________________ .

4. The new world champion body builder told the reporters that she had to leave : ______________________________

   ______________________________ .

5. ______________________________ :

   we toured the National Air and Space Museum, The Smithsonian Castle, and the new wing of the National Gallery of Art .

As you read for class assignments or pleasure, watch for sentences that follow this pattern and add them below.

____

Sentences with series

What is a series?

When you see or hear the word *series,* what comes immediately to mind? The World Series? A bowling series? A television series? A serial story in a magazine? Now let's think about how the word *series* applies to sentence structure.

A series is a group of three similar items, all of which go in the same slot of the sentence. All items in the series must be similar in form (all nouns or all verbs and so on) because they have the same grammatical function. You may have a series in any slot of the sentence: three or four verbs for the same subject; three or four objects for the same preposition; three or four adjectives or nouns in the object or complement slot. You may have a series with any part of speech, not only with single words but also with phrases or dependent clauses. You may have more than three items in a series, and you may also arrange them in different patterns:

A , B , C　　　A and B and C　　　A , B , and C

or with paired items:

A and B　　　C and D　　　E and F

Remember to use commas between the items of all series.

When is a series helpful?

A series is a good way to eliminate wordiness. If, for example, you have three short sentences, reduce them to a single sentence with a series somewhere in it.

PATTERN 4: A SERIES WITHOUT A CONJUNCTION
(a series in any part of the sentence)

A , B , C ______________________________ .

EXPLANATION:

This pattern is the simplest form of the series. The items are separated by commas, and in this special pattern there is no conjunction linking the final two items. Omitting this conjunction is effective, for it gives your sentence a quick, staccato sound.

Develop your ear!

Read the series aloud so that you hear whether the items flow together smoothly and euphoniously *without* the conjunction before the last item. Remember that tone and sound and fluency are important considerations here. Remember that each item should receive equal emphasis. None is more important than the others.

EXAMPLES:

The goals of the ecology-awareness movement are clear: breathable air, drinkable water, livable space, viable soil, potable waterways. (Note: A complete sentence comes before the colon.)

The coach is loud, profane, demonstrative; he has again been trapped, caught, humiliated.

The attorney impeached her own credibility, misrepresenting the record, divining meanings that only she perceived, discovering motives that only she comprehended, denying the undeniable.

The world of art is as universal as the wall paintings of primitive man, as varied as Picasso's talent, as fleeting as some modern art, as enduring as Rembrandt.

Shortly after midnight in a serene, enchanting, mysterious performance, the night-blooming cereus gradually begins to blossom.

With wisdom, patience, virtue, Queen Victoria directed the course of nineteenth-century England.

The United States has a government of the people, by the people, for the people.

"Guerin sat high on the concrete bank at freeway side, staring idly down upon the river of traffic beneath him: automobiles, taxis, panel trucks, dunebuggies with whiplash antennae, besurfboarded woodies, 24- and 32-wheeled big irons, groaning beer trucks and cement mixers, even an occasional police cruiser or wailing ambulance rolled below. . . ."

—Les Standiford, "Guerin and the Sail Cat Blues"

CHECKPOINTS:

✔ Since any part of the sentence may have a series, you must take care to make all items in the series parallel in form as they are already parallel in function.

Find the items that are not parallel in these awkward sentences:

The typical teenage user of snuff is white, active and athletic, and peer pressure is very heavy.

Swimming, surfing, to go boating—these were Sally's favorite sports at the summer camp.

Now explain why this revision is better:

Swimming, surfing, boating—these were Sally's favorite sports at the summer camp.

NOTE: Although it is not a pattern discussed in this book, you may want to remember that the commonest pattern for series—A , B , and C—should always have the comma before the conjunction; otherwise, the reader may be confused or may completely misread the meaning:

Shakespeare uses an image, a metaphor, a simile and rhyme scheme to clarify his theme in this sonnet. (A "simile and rhyme" scheme? Without the comma before the conjunction, that's what it says!)

The restaurant served four varieties of sandwiches: corned beef, pastrami, salami and egg with bacon. (Would you order the last one?)

EXERCISES:

Develop a series for each of the following sentences.

1. A theme traditionally has three major parts : ______________, ______________ ______________, ______________.

2. ______________, ______________ ______________, ______________ are my favorite summertime activities .

3. (Begin this sentence with three *-ed* words.) ______________, ______________ ______________, ______________, the gambler staggered away from the poker table with only a few coins in change .

4. (Provide a series of *-ing* words for the blanks.) The players formed a wide circle around the coach ______________ ______________, ______________, ______________.

5. After the announcement on the loudspeaker the rowdy spectators at the tennis match ______________, ______________, ______________ ______________.

As you read for class assignments or pleasure, watch for sentences that follow this pattern and add them below.

PATTERN 4a:	A SERIES WITH A VARIATION
A or B or C ________.	(in any place in the sentence)
A and B and C ________.	(in any place in the sentence)

EXPLANATION:

Occasionally, you will want to vary the previous pattern and instead write a series with conjunctions between all items (but usually not more than three). Again, let your ear be your guide. Listen for the tumbling rhythm in the following sentences.

EXAMPLES:

Peering down from the hill, Merlin could see the castle swathed in gloom and fear and death.

Despite his handicaps, I have never seen Larry angry or cross or depressed.

Many rodeo events lead to broken ribs or sprained knees or dislocated shoulders—or even worse.

Once you master the rhumba and the tango, you can turn to the more difficult South American dances like the samba or the cha-cha or the mambo.

"The fears of any diver in the water of Australia's Great Barrier Reef are obviously sharks and sea snakes and poisonous urchins." —T. White

"These sailboats vary widely in size and complexity and cost." —James Clay

R2D2 and C3P0, Mork and Mindy, Superman and Lois Lane, Popeye and Olive Oyl—all are known to youngsters and teenagers and grown-ups alike. (This sentence combines PATTERNS 4a, 5, and 6.)

"More than any of his competitors—Mike or Dick or John or Merv—Carson controls the life of every person who walks on his turf." —*TV Guide*

EXERCISES:

For the following incomplete sentences create series with conjunctions, omitting commas.

1. Looking toward Mount Franklin, I could see that the fading afternoon sun had tinted it ______________________ and ______________________ and ______________________ ______________ .

2. In order to win the television ratings war I suggest NBC drop ______________________ and ______________________ ________ and ______________________ .

3. ______________________ and ______________________ ______________ and ______________________ seem to be the issues in the Presidential campaign .

4. The professor asked the class: "What will be the predominant source of energy in the next decade: ______________ ______________ or ______________________ or ______________________?"

5. All that is ______________________ or ________ ______________ or ______________________ or ______________________ seems to be harmful to one's health .

Write sentences using the series listed below. In two of the sentences use no conjunctions between the items; in two of the sentences add a conjunction between each item.

1. spaghetti vermicelli ravioli macaroni

____

____

____

2. Milk for breakfast milk for lunch milk for dinner milk for a bedtime snack

____

____

____

3. baked potatoes boiled potatoes mashed potatoes

____

____

____

As you read for class assignments or pleasure, watch for sentences that follow this pattern and add them below.

____

____

____

____

____

PATTERN 5: A SERIES OF BALANCED PAIRS
(note the rhythm)

A and B , C and D , E and F .
(may be in any slot in the sentence)

EXPLANATION:

This pattern has a series with an *even* number of items—four or six or eight. Balance these in pairs with a conjunction between each of the paired items. This construction creates a balanced rhythm, but is this rhythm right for your sentence? Read the sentence aloud; listen to the cadence of your words because *rhythm* is the important feature of this pattern. Does your sentence have an orderly progression with a kind of climactic order for the items? Can you hear the items balanced against each other? Do you like the way the paired words sound together?

(NOTE: There are other coordinating conjunctions besides *and* and *or*. See second example below.)

EXAMPLES:

Anthony and Cleopatra, Romeo and Juliet, Lancelot and Guinevere were all famous lovers in literature.

Eager yet fearful, confident but somewhat suspicious, Jason eyed the barber who would give him his first haircut. (This is a variation of the pattern.)

"No man is really happy or safe without a hobby, and it makes precious little difference what the outside interest may be—botany, beetles, or butterflies; roses, tulips, or irises; fishing, mountaineering, or antiques—anything will do so long as he straddles a hobby and rides it hard." —Sir William Osler (Note that this sentence is a variation on a balanced series.)

"From Scott Joplin to the Beatles, Glen Miller to Elvis Presley, few things reflect the barometer of change in society as accurately as music." —*Harper's*

Motion picture history includes a number of famous screen pairs—Cheech and Chong, Newman and Redford, Smokey and the Bandit, Luke Skywalker and Princess Leia, Richard Burton and Elizabeth Taylor.

The author knew the distinctions that existed between liberals and conservatives, between vampires and vixens, between swashbucklers and the timid, between the exploited and the victimized.

"Before Uriah Heep I have step by step abandoned name and reputation, peace and quiet, house and home."

—*David Copperfield*

"Drawing on newspapers and other published accounts from that period, Penick lets those most affected—'male and female, educated and ignorant, preachers and sinners, scientists, rivermen, merchants, Indians and an undifferentiated assortment'—describe their brush with one of nature's fiercest forces." (This sentence, from a review of James Penick's *The New Madrid Earthquakes of 1811–1812,* combines PATTERNS 5, 12, and 11. Can you find any others?

EXERCISES:

Complete the following sentences. Fill in the appropriate blanks with a series of balanced pairs.

1. Martini or daiquiri , ______________________________ or

______________________________ , ______________________________

or ______________________________ — these are popular drinks .

2. If you are making up a list of popular comedians from film or television, you might want to consider my favorites:

______________________________ and ______________________________

__________ , ______________________________ and __________

__________ , ______________________________ and __________

______________________________ .

3. Americans choose both a president and a vice president every four years; in the past we have chosen from ____________

____________________ and ____________________

____________________ , ____________________ and

____________________ , ____________________

__________ and ____________________ .

4. Comic strip husbands and wives like ____________________

____________________ and ____________________

or ____________________ and ____________________

__________ provide ____________________ .

Compose three sentences to complete a balanced series pattern using the words listed below:

1. ham eggs coffee fruit toast jam

____

____

2. lions tigers leopards cheetahs

____

____

3. Halloween Thanksgiving Christmas New Year's Eve

____

____

As you read for class assignments or pleasure, watch for sentences that follow this pattern and add them below.

PATTERN 6: AN INTRODUCTORY SERIES OF APPOSITIVES
(with a dash and a summarizing subject)

Appositive , appositive , appositive — summary word S V .

(The key summarizing word before the subject may be one of these: *such, all, those, this, many, each, which, what, these, something, someone.* Sometimes this summary word will be the subject, but sometimes it will merely modify the subject.)

EXPLANATION:

This pattern begins with a "cluster" of appositives. An appositive is simply another word for something named elsewhere in the sentence—that is, it is another naming for some noun. After the appositives, there is a dash followed by a summarizing word and the subject—verb combination for the main clause. This word must sum up the appositives before it. You may arrange these appositives in any of the patterns for series (see PATTERNS 4, 4a, and 5).

This pattern produces a highly stylized sentence that is extremely effective for special places in your writing, places where you want to squeeze a lot of information into the same slot.

EXAMPLES:

The petty, the wronged, the fallen, the cowardly, the righteous, the deluded, the rapacious, the unctuous—each played a role on the stage of Cervantes' vast human vision.

Vanity, greed, corruption—which serves as the novel's source of conflict?

The crack of the lion trainer's whip, the dissonant music of the calliope, the neighs of Arabian stallions—such sounds mean "circus" to all children.

Foresight, humor, wit—all are evident in Omar Khayyam's *Rubiayat.*

Bull riding, camel races, bronc riding and roping—these events mean "rodeo" to many people; they mean money to the cowboys. (This example is a combination of PATTERNS 1 and 6.)

Billy the Kid, Jesse James, Butch Cassidy—all have survived their reported historic deaths to live out their lives in quiet anonymity.

The "Mona Lisa," *La Vita Nuova,* the frescoes in the Sistine Chapel—what an imagination those Italians had!

or:—which of these is the best proof of the Italian imagination?

or:—many are the wonders of the Renaissance in Italy.

An old photograph, a haunting fragrance, a sudden view of a half-forgotten scene—something unexpectedly triggers our nostalgia for the past.

NOTE: Sometimes these appositives can be at the end. Try reversing any of the sentences above, following the example of the sentence below:

The tea tax, the lack of representation, the distance from the Mother Country, the growing sense of being a new and independent country—what do you think caused the American Revolution?

What do you think caused the American Revolution—the tea tax, the lack of representation, the distance from the Mother Country, or the growing sense of being a new and independent country?

CHECKPOINTS:

✔ Check the punctuation of this pattern:

1. there must be commas between the appositives in the series;
2. there must be a dash after the series.

✔ Check to see that there is a summary word at the beginning of the main clause.

✔ As in any series, all these appositives must be parallel in structure and in meaning.

EXERCISES:

Complete the following introductory appositives so that they logically attach to the independent clause.

1. ______________ , ______________ , ______________ — each of these men gave his life for his country .

2. To ______________ , to ______________ , to ______________ — such are the goals of the average American college graduate .

3. ______________ and ______________ , ______________ and ______________ , ______________ and ______________ — what glories of the ancient world remain !

Complete the sentence by writing appropriate summarizing words and independent clauses.

1. Alienation , loneliness , rejection — ______________
____
______________ .

2. Poetry and music , painting and sculpture , drama and

dance — ____

____.

3. Hot then cold , rainy then windy , humid then dry —

____

____.

As you read for class assignments or pleasure, watch for sentences that follow this pattern and add them below.

____

____

____

____

____

____

____

____

____

____

PATTERN 7: AN INTERNAL SERIES OF APPOSITIVES OR MODIFIERS
(enclosed by a pair of dashes or parentheses)

S	— OR (	appositive , appositive , appositive modifier , modifier , modifier	— OR)	V	.

EXPLANATION:

The first of the sentence (or the last) is not the only place where you may have a series of appositives or modifiers. Appositives will re-name and modifiers will describe something named elsewhere in the sentence. Any kind of series (see PATTERNS 4, 4a, and 5) may come between the subject—verb, between two subjects, somewhere in an inverted sentence (see PATTERNS 15 and 15a), and so on. Because this kind of series will be a dramatic interruption within the sentence and may even have commas, there *must* be a dash before and a dash after it.

EXAMPLES:

"Which famous detective (d.o.)—Sherlock Holmes or Nero Wolfe or Dick Tracy—will (s.) you (v.) take as your model?" the sergeant asked.

The necessary qualities (d.o.) for political life—guile, ruthlessness, and garrulity—he (s.) learned (v.) by carefully studying his father's life.

(These examples illustrate a variation of the pattern where the direct object precedes the subject—verb.)

My favorite red wines—Zinfandel, Cabernet Savignon, Pinot Noir—blend well in making California rosé wines.

Three basic fencing moves (the advance, the retreat, the lunge) demand careful balance by both fencers.

Many of the books kids enjoy reading *(Little Women, Treasure Island, The Arabian Nights)* portray women in traditional and often uncomplimentary roles.

A mystical law of nature tells us that the three things we desire most in life—happiness, freedom, and peace of mind—are always attained by giving them to someone else.

The much despised predators—mountain lions, timber wolves, and grizzly bears—have been shot, trapped, and poisoned so relentlessly for so long that they have nearly vanished from their old haunts.

CHECKPOINTS:

✔ Do you have two dashes? It takes not one, but TWO, to make a pair.

✔ Can you read a "complete sentence" even after you eliminate the interrupting appositive or modifier? In other words, does the sentence convey its message without the words between the dashes? If so, you have punctuated properly, for the function of the dashes is to mark an interrupter that could be omitted.

EXERCISES:

Add an internal series of modifiers or appositives to complete the following sentences.

1. Which famous television personality — ______________

______________ or ______________

or ______________ — do you think will win

this year's Emmy Award ?

2. The youthful knight — ______________ ,

______________ , and ______________

— entered the jousting contest to impress the princess he

hoped to marry .

3. Television commercials — ______________ and

______________ and ______________

— hammer ruthlessly on the viewer's mind .

Complete the following sentences by incorporating the internal appositives or modifiers as suggested.

1. ____ — sociology or psychology or economics or political science — ____ .

2. ____ — coordination , agility , speed — ____________________________ ____________ .

3. ____ — lasagna and ravioli , spaghetti and meatballs , spumoni and tortoni — ____ .

4. ____ — perfumed body , seductive smile , suntanned legs — ____ .

As you read for class assignments or pleasure, watch for sentences that follow this pattern and add them below.

____

____

____

____

____

PATTERN 7a: A VARIATION: A SINGLE APPOSITIVE OR A PAIR

S	— OR (OR ,	appositive	— OR) OR ,	V	.

(Use two dashes or parentheses or commas to enclose this appositive.)

EXPLANATION:

This pattern resembles PATTERN 7 except that it has only one or two items for the appositive instead of a full series. Here, the appositive may be a single word or a pair of words; it may or may not have modifiers. In this variation, there is also an interruption in thought immediately after the subject, but here the appositive can have a variety of effects, depending on your punctuation:

a pair of dashes will make the appositive dramatic;

parentheses will make it almost whisper;

a pair of commas will make it nearly inconspicuous because they are so ordinary.

EXAMPLES:

A sudden explosion—artillery fire—signaled the beginning of a barrage.

A familiar smell—fresh blood—assailed his jungle-trained nostrils.

The ultimate polluter—you and I, my friend—must share the burden and the guilt for having created this dirty world.

The officer slapped on a yachting cap—his trademark—and composed his face into the smiling mask of a Yankee politician. (Note that the appositive comes *after* the first verb (*slapped*) and *before* the second verb (*composed*).

Two phases in the creative process—discovery and invention—seem to reinforce each other.

His former wife (once a famous Philadelphia model) now owns a well-known boutique in the Bahamas.

A popular theory among climatologists (the Greenhouse effect) suggests how the earth's temperature remains warm enough for man, animals, and plants to prosper.

The slogan of the firm—"See Texas First"—helped promote tourism and a variety of commercial products.

The first man to walk on the moon, Neil Alden Armstrong, is a man whom the world will never forget.

CHECKPOINTS:

✔ Again, it takes not one, but TWO, to make a pair—two dashes, two parentheses, two commas.

EXERCISES:

Provide a missing appositive or complete the sentence:

1. The familiar cheer of the football team — ______________________ — began to appear on bumper stickers around the town .
2. ______________________ (my father and best friend) ______________________ ______________________ .
3. Those two bright colors — ______________________ ______________________ — are prominent in all of the artist's later paintings .
4. Two ancient skills of the artists — ______________________

____________________ — can never be successfully imitated by contemporary craftsmen .

5. _____________________________________ (filing for divorce) shocked the members of the country club .

Make up an original sentence using the following words as an interrupting appositive:

1. Christopher Columbus ______________________________

____

2. pineapple juice ___________________________________

____

3. allowance or pin money ____________________________

____

As you read for class assignments or pleasure, watch for sentences that follow this pattern and add them below.

PATTERN 8: DEPENDENT CLAUSES IN A PAIR OR IN A SERIES (at beginning or end of sentence)

If . . . , if . . . , if . . . , then S V ______ .

When . . . , when . . . , when . . . , S V ______ .

S V ______ that . . . , that . . . , that . . . .

(omit the third clause and have just two, if you wish)

EXPLANATION:

The preceding patterns have shown series with single words or phrases. This pattern shows a series with dependent clauses. All of the clauses in this series must be dependent; they must also be parallel in structure; they must express conditions or situations or provisions dependent upon the idea expressed in the main clause. The series of dependent clauses may come at the beginning or at the end of the sentence. You will normally have two or three clauses here; rarely will four or five sound graceful and smooth. Try not to struggle for style; be natural, relaxed, never forced.

This pattern is a very special one. Save it for special places, special functions. It is particularly helpful

1. at the end of a single paragraph to summarize the major points;
2. in structuring a thesis statement having three parts (or points);
3. in the introductory or concluding paragraphs to bring together the main points of a composition in a single sentence.

EXAMPLES:

Because it might seem difficult at first, because it may sound awkward or forced, because it often creates lengthy sentences where the thought "gets lost," this pattern seems forbidding to some writers, but it isn't all that hard; try it.

In Biology 3130 Stella learned that a hummingbird does not really hum, that a screech owl actually whistles, and that storks prefer to wade in water than fly around carrying tiny babies.

When he smelled the pungent odor of pine, when he heard the chatter of jays interrupting the silence, when he saw the startled doe, the hunter knew he had reached the center of the forest.

Whether one needs fantasy or whether one needs stark realism, the theater can become a Mecca.

Since he had little imagination and since he had even less talent, he was unable to get the position.

"If radio's slim fingers can pluck music out of the night and toss it over mountains and sea; if the petal-white notes from a violin are blown across the desert and the city's din; if songs, like crimson roses, are caught from thin blue air—why should mortals wonder if God hears prayer?"

—Marvin Drake, *Catholic Digest*

CHECKPOINTS:

✔ Don't think there must always be three dependent clauses here. Two will work in this pattern also.

✔ Whether you have only two or a full series of three or more, whether you have the clauses at the beginning or end of the sentence, you should arrange them in some order of increasing impact.

EXERCISES:

Fill in the blanks to construct logical dependent or independent clauses:

1. If your mother tells you to be home by nine, if ______________________________, or if ______________________________, you'd better follow your mother's wishes rather than your sister's or your friend's .

2. When ______________________________ ,

when the astronaut heard the explosion, when the air controller ______________________________ , then the flight crew ______________________________ ________ .

3. The landlord ______________________________ ________ because ______________________________ ________ , because ______________________________ ________ .

4. Whether you think ______________________________ ________ or whether you think ______________________________ , you ______________________________ .

5. The basketball coach shouted that the referee ______________________________ , that the other team's coach ______________________________ ________ , and that ______________________________ .

As you read for class assignments or pleasure, watch for sentences that follow this pattern and add them below.

____

____

____

Repetitions

What are repetitions?

A repetition is a restatement of a term; you may repeat the term once or several times within a sentence or a paragraph.

Why use repetitions?

Repetitions help to echo key words, to emphasize important ideas or main points, to unify sentences, or to develop coherence between sentences. Skillful repetitions of important words or phrases create "echoes" in the reader's mind: they emphasize and point out key ideas. Sometimes you will use these "echo words" in different sentences—even in different paragraphs—to help "hook" your ideas together.

How do you create repetitions?

Simply allow some important word to recur in a sentence or in a paragraph or even in different paragraphs. These "echo words" may come any place in the sentence: with the subjects or the verbs, with the objects or the complements, with prepositions or other parts of speech. You need not always repeat the exact form of the word; think of other forms the word may take, such as *freak* (noun), *freaking* (participle), *freaky* (adjective), *freakiness* (noun), *freakish* (adjective), *freakishly* and *freakily* (adverbs), and *freak-ishness* (noun).

Where are repetitions appropriate?

Repetitions are appropriate in two different places in the sentence:

1. the same word repeated in a different position in the same sentence (PATTERN 9);
2. the same word repeated in the *same* position (or "slot") of the sentence: for example, the same preposition repeated in a series or the same word used as object of different prepositions (PATTERN 9a).

How does punctuation affect the repetition?

Commas, dashes, periods, colons, and semicolons signal varying degrees of pause. A comma makes a brief pause, whereas a dash signals a longer pause. There is a ring of finality in the pauses created by the colon, the semicolon, and the period. The colon suggests the important words will follow, whereas the semicolon (like the period) is an arresting mark of punctuation signaling a full stop before another idea begins.

You have probably noticed that, in all explanations (including the graphs that introduce each pattern), spacing before and after punctuation marks has been deliberately exaggerated so that you will pay attention to the important punctuation mark. When you imitate each pattern, however, you will want to use traditional spacing before and after punctuation marks. This spacing appears in all example sentences. If you are typing your papers, remember to space twice after the colon (:) and use two hyphen marks to distinguish a **dash** (—) from a **hyphen** (-).

When choosing between a comma and a dash, use this guideline to determine the type of pause you need: a **comma** signals a very brief pause (it's as though you have hiccupped right in the middle of your thought); a **dash** makes you take a longer breath. A period, colon, question mark, or exclamation mark makes you pause, take a deep breath, then allows you to continue.

Consider these differences; decide what kind of pause you need; then punctuate, remembering that these marks are not really interchangeable. Each one suggests a different kind of pause.

NOTE: Once you have mastered repetitions in the same sentence, you will be ready to repeat some key words or phrases throughout your paragraphs, even from one paragraph to the next. In your reading, look for the many ways that writers effectively repeat some of their key words, scattering them around at various places in the sentence and in different places throughout the same paragraph. In one paragraph Rachel Carson, for example, used "sea" ten times; Winston Churchill repeated the phrase "we shall fight" eight times, using it to emphasize various points throughout one dramatic speech.

PATTERN 9: REPETITION OF A KEY TERM

S V key term — OR , repeated key term . . . .

(use dash or comma before repetition)

EXPLANATION:

In this pattern you will repeat a key word in a modifying phrase attached to the main clause. You may repeat the word exactly as it is, or you may use another form of it: *brute* may become *brutal; breath* may become *breathtaking; battle* may become *battling.*

A key term is a word important enough to be repeated. It can come anywhere in the sentence, but the repetition is most common toward the end. Or, if you have a key word in the subject slot of the sentence, the repetition may be, for example, a part of an interrupting modifier.

You may also vary this pattern slightly by using a dash instead of a comma; remember that the dash suggests a longer pause, a greater break in thought than the comma permits.

NOTE NUMBER ONE:

Be sure that the word is worthy of repetition. Notice how ineffective the following "little Lulu" sentence is, and all because of the repetition of an uninteresting, overworked word.

> He was a good father, providing a good home for his good children.

NOTE NUMBER TWO:

Be sure that the attached phrase with the repeated key term is NOT a complete sentence; if it is, you will inadvertently create a comma splice, as here:

> He was a cruel brute of a man, he was brutal to his family and even more brutal to his friends.

Here's one way of correcting the comma splice:

> He was just a cruel brute of a man, brutal to his family and even more brutal to his friends.

EXAMPLES:

We all inhabit a mysterious, inorganic world—the inner world, the world of the mind.

A. E. Housman used this PATTERN 9 at the end of a famous lecture: "The tree of knowledge will remain forever, as it was in the beginning, a tree to be desired to make one wise."

In "The Lottery" Shirley Jackson mocks community worship of outworn customs, customs that no longer have meaning, customs that deny man his inherent dignity and link him with the uncivilized world of beasts.

Neither the warning in the tarot cards—an ominous warning about the dangers of air flight—nor the one on her ouija board could deter Marsha from volunteering for the first Mars shot.

Looking into the cottage we saw great splotches of blood smeared on the walls, walls that only that morning had rung with shouts of joy and merriment.

CHECKPOINTS:

✔ ✔ Double check! Notice that the repetition is in a phrase, not a clause. In this pattern, the words following the comma MUST NOT have a subject or a verb with the repeated word; the result would be a comma splice (comma fault).

WRONG: He was part of the older generation, his generation was born before the depression. (This compound must have a semicolon).

CORRECT: He was part of the older generation, a generation born before the depression.

A common error occurs when there is a period or semicolon where the comma should be, thereby creating a fragment out of the modifier containing the repeated key term.

WRONG: He praises the beauty of his love. A love that is unfortunately hopeless because it is not mutual.

CORRECT: He praises the beauty of his love, a love unfortunately hopeless because it is not mutual.

NOTE: The first example contains the "pattern" of a very common fragment error:

S V . S + [dep. clause] but NO verb .

EXERCISES:

Complete the following sentences by repeating the underlined words.

1. The destruction caused by the tornado was devastating , devastating to ______________________________ , devastating also to ______________________________ ______________________________ .

2. Ruthless — ruthless to ______________________________ ____________ , ruthless to ______________________________ ______________ — the leader of the insurgents showed no mercy to the unlucky civilians who lived in the community .

3. The faithful worshipers believed the religious leader to be a loving man , ______________________________ .

Develop original sentences repeating a word that ends in *-ing*.

1. ______________________________
____

2. ______________________________

____

As you read for class assignments or pleasure, watch for sentences that follow this pattern and add them below.

____

____

____

____

____

____

____

____

____

____

PATTERN 9a:	A VARIATION: SAME WORD REPEATED IN PARALLEL STRUCTURE

S V repeated 1 key word in same position of the sentence .

EXPLANATION:

Repetitions of words may occur in other ways, of course.

A. You may want to repeat some effective adjective or adverb in phrases or clauses with parallel construction:

That South Pacific island is an *isolated* community, *isolated* from the values of the West, *isolated* from the spiritual heritage of the East.

B. You may repeat the same preposition in a series:

All revolutionists are negative; they are *against* things—*against* the values of the present and *against* the traditions of the past, *against* materialism and *against* mysticism, *against* taxation and representation and legislation.

C. You may repeat the same noun as the object of different prepositions:

This government is of the *people,* by the *people,* and for the *people.*

D. You may repeat the same modifying word in phrases that begin with different words:

Sidney devoted his life to those *selfish* people, for their *selfish* cause, but clearly with his own *selfish* motives dominating his every action.

E. You may repeat the same intensifiers:

Audrey appeared *very* chic, *very* classic, *very* blasé.

Politicians sometimes concern themselves with *some* important issues, *some* burning questions, *some* controversy dear to their constituents.

F. You may repeat the same verb or alternate forms of the same word:

"It isn't always others who enslave us. Sometimes we let circumstances enslave us; sometimes we let routine enslave us; sometimes we let things enslave us; sometimes, with weak wills, we enslave ourselves."

—Richard Evans, *Richard Evans' Quote Book*

EXAMPLES:

"Porphyria's Lover" captures a moment of time, a moment of passion, a moment of perverse indulgence.

His greatest discoveries, his greatest successes, his greatest influence upon the world's daily life came to Edison after repeated failure.

"Villainy is the matter; baseness is the matter; deception, fraud, conspiracy are the matter. . . . "

—*David Copperfield*

Taylor entered his sophomore year with renewed hope, renewed enthusiasm, renewed determination not to repeat the errors of his freshman year.

You must find other ambitions, other goals if your first ones don't work out.

"The book sprawls and passes its perfect happy ending, where the lovers, at last free to marry, at last accepted by the public, at last secure that their romance will not destroy their careers, reach the final consummation of sharing a bag of popcorn at a movie." —Joan Quarm

EXERCISES:

Expand the following basic sentences by repeating one of the modifying words in a phrase.

1. Your grandmother was right : there is nothing new under the sun , nothing ______________________________

__________ , only ______________________________________

__________ .

2a. But these numbers tell only part of the story , only

____ , only

____ , only

____ .

b. (Rewrite the same sentence but this time repeat the word "part.") But these numbers tell only part of the story , part

____ , part

____ .

3a. The western world possesses awesome amounts of virtually untapped resources , awesome ______________________

______________________ , awesome ______________________

______________________ .

b. (Rewrite the same sentence but repeat "untapped.") The western world possesses awesome amounts of virtually untapped resources , untapped ______________________

______________________ , untapped ______________________ .

c. (Rewrite the same sentence but this time repeat the word "resources.") The western world possesses awesome amounts of virtually untapped resources , ________________

____ , resources

____ , resources ______________________________,

resources ______________________________.

As you read for class assignments or pleasure, watch for sentences that follow this pattern and add them below.

____

____

____

____

____

____

____

____

____

____

PATTERN 10: EMPHATIC APPOSITIVE AT END, AFTER A COLON

S V word : the appositive (the second naming) .
(with or without modifiers)

EXPLANATION:

Often it is an idea, not a word, that you wish to repeat. Withholding it until the end builds the sentence to a climax and provides a pattern for a forceful, emphatic appositive at the end of the sentence where it practically shouts for your reader's attention. In the above pattern, the colon—because it is formal and usually comes before a rather long appositive—emphasizes this climax. Remember that the colon makes a full stop and therefore must come only after a complete statement; it tells the reader that important words or an explanation will follow.

EXAMPLES:

Atop the back of the lobster is a collection of trash: tiny starfish, moss, pieces of kelp, sea conchs, crabs.

"Lobsters are also vulnerable to a variety of other dooms: shell disease, gill disease, gas disease, plug rot, and epidemics of *red tail.*" —Alexander Theroux

A soldier who goes AWOL has one particular concern: to hide from the MP's.

Anyone left abandoned on a desert should avoid two dangers: cactus needles and rattlesnakes.

Were those twins my children, I'd make one thing clear to them: the curfew hour.

CHECKPOINTS:

✓ Check the words *before* the colon; be sure they make a full statement (sentence).

✓ After the colon, be sure to write only a word or a phrase—not a full statement (sentence). See PATTERN 3.

EXERCISES:

Supply the missing parts for the following sentences. Each sentence should include an emphatic appositive.

1. ____ :

   an "A," the grade I really had hoped for .

2. (Make up a sentence with a person's name as the emphatic appositive.) ______________________________

   __________ : ________________________
   (name)

3. The class elected ______________________________

   ________ as treasurer : Jim Rutledge .

4. ______________________________________ award :

   ________________________ , the most coveted of all

   ________________________ distinctions .

5a. (Make up a sentence with an emphatic single-word appositive. After the appositive use a prepositional phrase to modify it.) ______________________________________ :

   ____ .
   (appositive plus prepositional phrase)

b. (Rewrite the sentence in *a* and make the emphatic appositive into an infinitive phrase. Remember that an infinitive begins with *to* and the base form of the verb, as in *to squirm*.)

   ____ :

   to ____ .
   (infinitive phrase)

c. (Now repeating the same idea as in *a* and *b* above, modify the emphatic appositive with a word group beginning with *-ing* or an *-ed* word—that is, a *present* or *past* tense participle.)

______ : ________________________________ .
(*-ing* or *-ed* word)

As you read for class assignments or pleasure, watch for sentences that follow this pattern and add them below.

____

____

____

____

____

____

____

____

____

____

PATTERN 10a:	A VARIATION: APPOSITIVE (single or pair or series) AFTER A DASH

S V word — the appositive . . . .
(echoed idea or second naming)

EXPLANATION:

For variation, for a more informal construction, you may use a dash instead of a colon before a short, emphatic appositive at the end of a sentence. Notice that in both PATTERNS 10 and 10a, the second naming is usually climactic or emphatic. The difference is only in punctuation: a dash almost always precedes a short, climactic appositive, whereas a colon generally precedes longer appositives. (Now contrast PATTERN 9 with PATTERN 10a.)

Study the difference in sound and emphasis that punctuation and the length of the appositive make in the following sentences:

A new job requires one quality, humor.
(common usage but not emphatic) BLAH!

Adjusting to a new job requires one quality above all others—a sense of humor. (dramatic signaling)

Adjusting to a new situation requires one quality: humor.
(significant pause, but not so dramatic)

Adjusting to a new job requires one quality: the ability to laugh at oneself. (more dramatic, more stylistically complete)

EXAMPLES:

Most contemporary philosophies echo ideas of one man—Plato.

The relatively few salmon that do make it to the spawning grounds have another old tradition to deal with—male supremacy.

The grasping of sea weeds reveals the most resourceful part of the sea horse—its prehensile tail.

But now there is an even more amazing machine simplifying man's daily life—the microcomputer.

No matter how reticent the players may be they will always have someone with a lust for commanding center stage—the coach.

The Greeks' defeat by Alexander could have been averted if they had listened to their most astute statesman—Demosthenes, the brilliant adviser of the Athenians.

CHECKPOINTS:

✔ The second naming must be a true appositive; don't simply "stick in" a dash or a colon before you get to the end of the sentence. If you do, you may have simply an error in punctuation, not a true appositive. Here is an example, lifted from a student's paper:

POOR: One class of teenagers can be labeled—students.

CORRECT: One label would fit almost any teenager: student.

EXERCISES:

Rewrite the following sentences so that they end with a dramatic appositive after a dash. You may need to add, delete, or rearrange words.

1. *War and Peace,* one of the world's great masterpieces, covers Napoleon Bonaparte's crucial campaign, an invasion of Russia by the largest army ever assembled from twenty nations.

____

____

____

2. The thesis of *War and Peace,* as stated by Tolstoy, is that the course of the greatest historical events is determined ulti-

mately not by the military leaders, but by the common, ordinary people.

____

____

____

Compose or rewrite sentences as directed below:

1. (Supply the missing dramatic appositive.) The destiny of nations is controlled by the common people — __________
____ .

2a. (Make up a sentence ending with a dramatic single-word appositive after a dash.) ______________________________
______________ — ______________________________ .
(single word)

b. (Rewrite the sentence but this time create a dramatic prepositional phrase to end it.) ______________________________
______________ — ______________________________
(prepositional phrase)
____ .

c. (Again rewrite the sentence ending it with a dramatic infinitive phrase.) ______________________________________
— ____ .
(infinitive phrase)

d. (Now repeat the same idea using an *-ing* or an *-ed* word or phrase at the beginning of the dramatic appositive.)
____ —
____ .
(*-ing* or *-ed* word here)

As you read for class assignments or pleasure, watch for sentences that follow this pattern and add them below.

____

____

____

____

____

____

____

____

____

____

Modifiers

Adding modifiers is a good way to clarify a sentence that is too brief or lean. Often some key word will require additional explanation—modifiers—in order to make its meaning clear. Modifiers are especially helpful if you wish to appeal to your reader's senses, to add some figurative language, or to make comparisons or allusions.

These modifiers may be single words, phrases, even clauses; they may be at the beginning, in the middle, or at the end of the sentence. They may be ideas or descriptions or figures of speech. Take two short, ineffective sentences. Make one into a modifier or a dependent clause, and then combine it with the other sentence for a stronger, clearer construction.

You will have no trouble with modifiers if you remember one fact: like leeches or magnets, they cling to the nearest possible target. Therefore, take care to avoid misplaced or dangling modifiers. If they cling to the wrong target, you will have an incoherent or illogical or ludicrous sentence.

PATTERN 11: INTERRUPTING MODIFIER BETWEEN S — V

S	,	modifier	,	V	.
S	—	modifier	—	V	.
S	(	modifier that whispers	)	V	.

EXPLANATION:

When the modifier comes *between* the subject and the verb, you may use a pair of commas or a pair of dashes to separate it from the main elements of the sentence. If the modifier is merely an aside within the sentence (a kind of whisper), put parentheses around it for variety in punctuation. This modifier need not be just a single word; it may be a pair of words or even a phrase.

EXAMPLES:

A small drop of ink, falling like dew upon a thought, can make millions think.

A small drop of ink, falling (as Byron said) like dew upon a thought, can make millions think.

His manner—pompous and overbearing to say the least—was scarcely to be tolerated.

Wolves (once common throughout North America) are now almost extinct.

To be only a street musician and nothing else—like an organ grinder or a gypsy fiddler—was an outrage Greg's family could not tolerate.

Rodeo bullriding contests—while they look tougher—are really easier to qualify for than saddle-bronc riding.

NOTE: Interrupting modifiers may also come at some point other than between the subject and verb. See the following examples.

He jumped at the chance (too impetuously, really) to shoot the rapids in his kayak.

CB radio is illegal—even for walkie-talkies—in Belgium. (Note how the modifier *follows* the verb and its complement.)

The coach has this habit (at tense moments) of throwing his heavy clipboard. (Here the modifier follows the verb and its direct object.)

CHECKPOINTS:

✔ The punctuation marks for this pattern must go in pairs, with one mark before the modifier and a matching mark after it.

EXERCISES:

Add additional information and descriptions of the subjects in the following sentences by providing missing interrupting *modifiers* or other missing parts. (Review your exercises for PATTERNS 7 and 7a and have a clear idea of the difference between an interrupting appositive and an interrupting modifier before you begin this exercise.)

1. My Father's day gift — ______________________________

__________ — ______________________________ .

2. ______________________________ — like the amber of a stunning topaz — ______________________________

______________________________ .

3. ______________________________ — distressing yet not unexpected — ______________________________

______________________________ .

4. The gestures of the orchestra leader — ______________________________

______________________________ — were almost

______________________________ .

5. (Use this sentence for the exercises below.) The political candidate learned the results of the Michigan primary.

   a. (Provide **one** or **two** words ending in *-en* as the interrupting modifier.) The political candidate , ____________________ ____________________ , learned the results of the Michigan primary .

   b. (Provide **two** words ending in *-ing* as the interrupting modifier.) The political candidate — ____________________ ____________________ — learned the results of the Michigan primary .

   c. (Provide a modifier in **parentheses** that whispers.) The political candidate (____________________ ________) learned the results of the Michigan primary

As you read for class assignments or pleasure, watch for sentences that follow this pattern and add them below.

____

____

____

____

____

____

____

PATTERN 11a:	A FULL SENTENCE AS INTERRUPTING MODIFIER (statement or question or exclamation)

S — a full sentence — **OR** (a full sentence) V .

EXPLANATION:

The modifier that interrupts the main thought expressed by the subject—verb combination may be more than merely words or phrases. It may be a full sentence, a full question, or an exclamation. If it is a full sentence, do not put a period before the second dash unless the sentence is a quotation. If it is a question or an exclamation, however, you will need punctuation. A question mark or an exclamation point may seem strange in the middle of a sentence, but this pattern requires such punctuation.

The interrupting modifier need not always come between the subject and the verb, it may come in other places in the sentence (see the last three examples below). And notice the different signals that the punctuation gives the reader: parentheses really say that the material enclosed is simply an aside, not very important; the dashes, however, say that the interrupter is important to a full understanding of some word in the sentence.

EXAMPLES:

An important question about education—should universities teach the classics or just courses in science and practical subjects?—was the topic of a famous debate by Arnold and Huxley.

Juliet's most famous question—early in the balcony scene she asks, "Wherefore art thou Romeo?"—is often misunderstood; she meant not "where" but "why."

One of Thoreau's most famous metaphors—"If a man does not keep pace with his companions, perhaps it is because he hears a different drummer. Let him step to the music which he hears, however measured or far away."—echoes Shakespeare's advice that each man should be true to himself.

Amy's pets—she says that any animal that waits by her refrigerator for a snack surely qualifies as a pet—are insured for $10,000.

He jumped at the chance (too impetuously, I thought) to shoot the rapids in his kayak. (Here the interrupting modifier comes *after* the verb.)

Although I was standing on the rolling slopes wearing my new $500 ski outfit—I was pretending I knew how to ski—I never dared to ski down.

Narcissus ignored Echo so completely (how could he? she was such a lovely nymph!) that she just faded away.

CHECKPOINT:

✔ Use this pattern with restraint. Otherwise your reader may think you have a "grasshopper mind" and never finish one thought without interference from another thought.

EXERCISES:

Supply the missing parts for these sentences, keeping in mind that for this pattern the modifier must be a sentence.

1. The scary movie (I know ____________________

__________ !) ______________________________ .

2. Julius Caesar's famous question — "Et tu Brute?" —

____ .

3. My new Florida suntan — ____________________

__________ — seemed out of place for January in Buffalo's

blizzards .

4. ________________________________ (it dates

back to the 1950's, at least) ______________________________

____.

5. Normally thought to be of Dutch origin, the tulip — ______________________________ — originally came from central Asia .

As you read for class assignments or pleasure, watch for sentences that follow this pattern and add them below.

____

____

____

____

____

____

____

____

____

____

PATTERN 12:		INTRODUCTORY OR CONCLUDING PARTICIPLES	
Participial phrase	,	S V	.
S V	,	Participial phrase	.

EXPLANATION:

Modifiers come in a variety of forms—single words, groups of words, even clauses. One interesting kind of modifier is the participial modifier, a verb form that is a modifier instead of a verb. There are three types of participles:

present (ending in *-ing*)

past (normally ending in *-ed*)

irregular (so *irregular* that you will have to memorize these!)

EXAMPLE: Persevering, determined to succeed, blest with discipline, the pioneers forged a civilization out of a wilderness.

Persevering (present regular)

determined (past regular)

blest (past irregular)

The dictionary will help you with all participial forms. Remember that they all function as adjectives; that is, they modify nouns or words working as nouns.

Once you understand what a participle is, this pattern is simple. It shows participial modifiers at the beginning and at the end of the sentence, though of course they may also come as interrupters at any point in the sentence (see the first two examples under PATTERN 11).

CAUTION: Don't dangle participles! Give them something logical to attach themselves to. You will have no trouble with them if you remember not to "shift subjects" at the comma: the idea or person you describe in the modifying phrase, not some other person or word, must be the subject of your sentence. Inadvertent danglers sometimes result in unintentional humor or illogical statements:

Walking onto the stage, the spotlight followed the singer.

Overgrown with moss, the gardener cleaned his seed flats for spring planting. ("Overgrown with moss" is the participial phrase here.)

Mr. Brown became terrified and ran out of his house, leaving his wife, with his pajamas on.

The three boys tried to steal my bike while going on an errand.

The man in the advertisement is shown standing in the middle of a stream holding an axe surrounded by trees.

He stumbled over his feet taking off his pants in the door.

When browned and bubbling, remove the pie from the oven.

See examples below for modifiers that don't dangle.

EXAMPLES:

Chaucer's monk is quite far removed from the ideal occupant of a monastery, given as he was to such pleasures as hunting, dressing in fine clothes, and eating like a gourmet. ("Given" is the participle here.)

Overwhelmed by the tear gas, the rioters groped their way toward the fountain to wash their eyes.

The wrangler reached for his lasso, knowing he must help to corral the straying steers.

Printed in Old English and bound in real leather, the new edition of *Beowulf* was too expensive for the family to buy. ("Printed" and "bound" are the participles here.)

Having once been burned on a hot stove, the cat refused to go into the kitchen.

Appearing on television talk shows, crisscrossing the country on the campus lecture circuit, invited to be on the programs of important symposia, fad theorists become the darlings of our society before we forget and discard them for others.

EXERCISES:

Try these exercises:

1. (Rewrite the following sentence, beginning it with an *-ed* word.) If you water your African violets carefully, they will burst into bloom. ______________________________

____

2. (Rewrite the following sentence, beginning it with an *-ed* word.) The underdog team, the Mets, beat the Hawks, but the Hawks won the championship cup in May. ____________

____

3. (Supply the missing words in this sentence. Begin with an *-ing* word.) ____________________________________, the prisoner escaped to freedom .

4. (Begin the following sentence with an *-ed* word. Follow the *-ed* word with one *-ly* modifier.) ____________________, the child finally dozed off to sleep .

5. (Supply the missing words in the sentence. Begin with an *-ing* word. Follow the *-ing* word with an *-ly* word.) ______ ________________________, the sparrow darted from the lower branch to the top of the tree .

6. (Rewrite the following sentence with a participial phrase at the *end* of the sentence.) The residents of the apartment obeyed the water restriction rule only because they watered the lawn on Thursdays. ______________________________

____

____

7. (Supply the missing words in this sentence. Begin the missing word group with an *-ing* word.) Spring weather always brightens my spirits ____________________ ing

____________________ .

As you read for class assignments or pleasure, watch for sentences that follow this pattern and add them below.

____

____

____

____

____

____

____

____

PATTERN 13:	A SINGLE MODIFIER OUT OF PLACE FOR EMPHASIS

Modifier .... , S V .

(modifier may be in other positions)

EXPLANATION:

If you wish to place additional emphasis on any modifier, put it somewhere other than its normal place in the sentence. Sometimes in this new position the modifier seems so normal that it sounds clear without a comma; at other times, you *must* have a comma to keep the reader from misinterpreting your sentence. For example:

As a whole, people tend to be happy.
(Otherwise, "As a whole people . . . .")

To begin with, some ideas are difficult.
(To begin with some ideas?)

Sometimes a single word like "before," "inside," or "below" may look like a preposition instead of an adverb if you forget the comma in a sentence like this one:

Inside, the child was noisy.

Now look what internal rumblings you create when you have no comma:

Inside the child was noisy. (It *was?*)

If the modifier is clearly an adverb, however, you may not need the comma:

Later the child was quiet.

Using this pattern may help you to avoid another pitfall in writing sentences—the split infinitive. In the following sentence "occasionally" would be better at the beginning than where it is, separating the two parts of the infinitive. And "further" should follow "illustrate."

Francesca liked to *occasionally wade* in the neighbor's pool.

The professor tried to *further illustrate* the point of the essay.

EXAMPLES:

Below, the traffic looked like a necklace of ants.

Frantically, the young mother called for help.

Frantic, the young mother rushed out the door with the baby in her arms.

All afternoon the aficionados sweltered on the sunny side of the corrida watching the matador from Mexico City, their latest idol.

The general demanded absolute obedience, instant and unquestioning.

Bert decided long ago to be a soldier of fortune.

The autumn leaves, burgundy red and fiery orange, showered down like a cascade of butterflies.

EXERCISES:

Revise the following sentences so that a modifier you want to emphasize comes at the beginning.

1. Rodeos began as rough-and-ready contests among rival cowboys to settle long festering differences. ____________

____

____

2. Rodeos are a multi-million-dollar business now in all parts of the West. ____________________________

____

____

3. Many rodeo events lead to black eyes, broken ribs, dislocated shoulders, or even worse injuries. ______

______

______

4. Saddle-bronc riding, which requires coordination, balance, timing, is naturally considered the classic rodeo event.

______

______

5. The inmates of the Huntsville prison organize a well-publicized, rough-and-tumble rodeo every October. ______

______

______

As you read for class assignments or pleasure, watch for sentences that follow this pattern and add them below.

______

______

______

______

______

______

______

______

Inversions

Not all sentences need to start with the traditional subject—verb combination. For variety you may wish to invert the normal order by beginning the sentence with a modifier out of its normal place; complements or direct objects may occasionally precede the subject. These inverted units may be single words, phrases, or dependent clauses.

Be wary of any inverted pattern, however. It might lead to awkwardness if your writing is undisciplined. Inverting the natural order should always result in a graceful sentence, not one that seems forced or like an intentional gimmick. Just as every sentence should seem natural, almost inevitable in its arrangement, so too must the one that departs from traditional sentence order. Try not to call attention deliberately to any inversion; make it fit into the context gracefully. Aim for sentences that possess the magic of variety, yes; but remember that too much variety, too obviously achieved, may be worse than none at all. (Turn to PATTERN 15a for further explanation.)

PATTERN 14: PREPOSITIONAL PHRASE BEFORE S — V

Prepositional phrase .... S V (or V S) ________________ .

EXPLANATION:

Before trying this pattern, remember what a preposition is. The very name indicates its function: it has a "*pre*-position." The "pre" means that it comes before an object, which is necessary to make a prepositional phrase. In other words, a preposition never occurs alone because it must show the relationship between the word it modifies and its own object. For example, consider a box and a pencil. Where can you put the pencil in relation to the box? It might be "on the box" or "under the box," "in the box" or "near the box," "inside the box" or "beside the box." Can you think of other prepositions?

For this pattern, put the prepositional phrase at the beginning of the sentence, making sure that the inversion emphasizes the modifying phrase without sounding awkward. Only your ear will tell you whether to put a comma after it; will the reader need the punctuation for easy reading? If so, provide it.

For example, these sentences *must* have commas:

After that, time had no meaning for him.
Beyond this, man can probably never go.
(Not "after that time" or "beyond this man.")

These sentences do well without a comma:

Until next summer there will be no more swimming.
During the winter months Tom worked as a trapper.

EXAMPLES:

For every season of the year there is some magic, some unique delight.

Down the field and through the tacklers ran Herschel Walker.

Despite his Master's degree in World Trade and Economics, the only job Chester could get was making change in an Atlantic City casino.

With slow and stately cadence the honor guard entered the Windsor castle grounds.

Into the arena rushed the brave bulls to defy death and the matador.

In all the forest no creature stirred.

CHECKPOINTS:

✓ Sometimes a comma is necessary after the prepositional phrase, sometimes not. Let the sound and meaning of your sentence guide you.

EXERCISES:

Supply the missing parts of these sentences that include introductory prepositional phrases. Try to use *more* than one or two words in each blank.

1. To the athletes ______________________________ ________, the new NCAA regulations represented ______________________________.

2. ______________________________ stood the farmer holding a loaded shot gun .

3. After ______________________________ yet before ______________________________, the veterans soon realized that ______________________________ ______________.

4. In ______________________________ by ______________________________ of ______

________ the Persian cat ______________________________

________.

5. With a clear ______________________________________

________ of the principles of ________________________

________ , a student __________________________________

____.

As you read for class assignments or pleasure, watch for sentences that follow this pattern and add them below.

____

____

____

____

____

____

____

____

____

____

PATTERN 15:	OBJECT OR COMPLEMENT BEFORE S — V

Object or Complement S V ________________.

EXPLANATION:

Occasionally you may wish to invert and thereby stress some part of the sentence that ordinarily comes after the verb (the direct object or the subject complement). These may go at the beginning of the sentence instead of in their normal positions. This inversion adds invisible italics to the part of the sentence you write first. When you use this pattern, always read your inversion aloud to be sure that it sounds graceful in context, that it blends well with the other sentences around it. Here, as in the preceding PATTERN 14, only the sound and rhythm of the sentence will indicate whether you need a comma or not; there are no rules.

EXAMPLES:

These examples have the direct object before the subject–verb combination:

His kind of sarcasm I do not like.

Celia's interest in tarot cards and Sammy's absorption in horoscopes Mrs. de la Renza could never understand.

These examples have a subject complement before the subject—verb combination:

The Tin Lizzie may have been the most dependable automobile of its day, but quiet it wasn't.

Prestige he can buy with his money; true friends he will never have.

No enemy of metaphor is Amy Lowell.

Famous and wealthy an English professor will never be.

"Up went the steps, bang went the door, round whirled the wheels, and off they rattled."
—Charles Dickens, *The Old Curiosity Shop*

CHECKPOINTS:

✔ Inversions are easy to do out of context, just for the exercise. But in a setting with your other sentences, you need to take care that they sound natural, not forced or awkward. Therefore use them sparingly, and then only for special emphasis.

EXERCISES:

Supply the missing information in these inverted sentences:

1. ______________________________ was Cinderella , but then neither were her step sisters .
2. ______________________________ a child seldom understands .
3. ______________________________ the Heiseman Trophy may always be , yet it remains a goal of all college football players .
4. The Congressional Medal of Honor every soldier ______________________________ ; however , few ______________________________ .
5. ______________________________ solar power might well become .

As you read for class assignments or pleasure, watch for sentences that follow this pattern and add them below.

____

PATTERN 15a:	COMPLETE INVERSION OF NORMAL PATTERN
Object OR Complement OR Modifier	V S .

EXPLANATION:

The standard English syntax is

subject—verb

subject—verb—modifier

subject—verb—completer (direct object or subject complement).

Completely reversing the order of these sentence parts will create an emphasis and a rhythm you can achieve in no other way:

verb—subject

modifier—verb—subject

completer—verb—subject.

This pattern will add spice to your prose; but like garlic or cayenne pepper, too much can be overpowering. So restrain yourself; don't overuse this pattern. It will probably fit better into dramatic statements or poetic prose passages than into business letters or laboratory reports.

EXAMPLES:

Westward the country was free;	Mod S V C
westward, therefore, lay their hopes;	Mod V S
westward flew their dreams. It became	Mod V S
for everyone the promised land of milk and honey.	Prep. phrase out of place between V and SC

From the guru's prophecy radiated a faith that ultimately all would be well.

Down the street and through the mist stumbled the unfamiliar figure.

Even more significant have been the criticisms about the quality of life in our affluent society.

In "The English Mail Coach" DeQuincey has a sentence with PATTERNS 15 and 15a: "But craven he was not: sudden had been the call upon him and sudden was his answer to the call."

From his years of suffering came eventual understanding and compassion.

CHECKPOINTS:

✔ This pattern must never offend the ear by sounding awkward or stilted.

✔ Test your sentence by reading it aloud. How does it sound?

✔ Is it consistent with your tone? Does it fit neatly into the context?

EXERCISES:

Revise the following sentences so that you create a complete inversion of the normal subject—verb pattern. You may have to add, delete, or alter some of the wording.

1. The gallant marine did not fear death. ____________________

____

2. When we fly to Europe, we must visit London and Paris and Rome. ____________________

____

3. Marching against the Mexican army, the brave Texans chanted, "Remember the Alamo!" ____________________

____

____

4. Man's power of choice, either for good or evil, is boundless.

____

5. The dreamer and the doer live side by side in each of us.

____

As you read for class assignments or pleasure, watch for sentences that follow this pattern and add them below.

____

____

____

____

____

____

____

____

____

____

An Assortment of Patterns

PATTERN 16:			PAIRED CONSTRUCTIONS		
Not only	S V	,	but also (The *also* may be omitted.)	S V	.
Just as	S V	,	so too (may be *so also* or simply *so*)	S V	.
If not	S V	,	at least	S V	.
The more	S V	,	the more (may be *the less*)	S V	.
The former	S V	,	the latter	S V	.

EXPLANATION:

Some words work in pairs; for example, "either" takes an "or"; "not only" takes "but also." These correlative conjunctions link words, phrases, or clauses that are similar in construction. The patterns in the box above illustrate some common phrases used for paired constructions that may occur in simple or in compound sentences. You will find this structure particularly helpful in making a comparison or a contrast.

Whenever you use this pattern, remember to make both parts of the construction parallel; that is, make them both have the same grammatical structure and rhythm.

EXAMPLES:

American tourists must realize that violations of laws in China are serious not only because they flaunt traditional codes of behavior but also because they reflect contempt for Oriental culture.

Just as wisdom cannot be purchased, so virtue cannot be legislated.

As things had begun, so they continued.

Reluctantly, every dieter looks for a favorable verdict from his bathroom scale; if not a pound less, at least not a pound more.

The more lay participation a parish in the Roman Catholic church has, the stronger it becomes for its parishioners.

"As in football, so in political campaigning, the aim is to roll up the numbers and win." —Herman Wouk, *Parade*

The more I eat chocolate fudge sundaes, the less I enjoy strawberry shortcake and other desserts.

Kai and Ernst were two of my favorite ski instructors: the former taught me downhill racing; the latter helped carry me to the hospital where Dr. Alexander set my fractured arm.

"Just as it remained for the public broadcasting system to show what television could do in the field of drama, so it has remained for PBS to show what the medium could do with history." —Cleveland Amory

CHECKPOINTS:

✔ Remember that "pair" means "two." Be sure you have the second part of the construction; don't give the reader a signal suggesting two items and then provide only one. To say "Not only is she pretty" and then say no more is to leave your reader confused.

MORE PAIRS: The following list of correlative conjunctions might further aid you in developing this pattern:

whether . . . or	so . . . that
such . . . that	not only . . . more than that
both . . . and	as . . . as
neither . . . nor	not so . . . as

CAUTION: Put both conjunctions of the pair in a logical place so that what follows each one will be parallel.

WRONG: The prisoner was [not only] found guilty of murder [but also] ↓ of robbery.
(no parallel verb here)

CORRECT: The prisoner was found guilty
not only of robbery
but also of murder.
(parallel construction;
better order for climax, too.)

WRONG: I not only forgot my keys
but also ↓ my purse.
(no parallel verb)

CORRECT: I forgot not only my keys
but also my purse.

EXERCISES:

Complete the following sentences with logically paired constructions.

1. The ______________________ Robert tried to please his fiancee the ______________________ dissatisfied ______________________.

2. The ______________________ a parent spends on a child's Christmas present the ______________________ ________ the child ______________________ ________.

3. Just as national public radio provides new opportunities to ______________________, so it ______________________.

4. The Mercedes Benz's beauty is ______________________ ________ in its design ______________________ ________ in its function .

5. ________________________________ if not the Pattersons , at least their neighbors .

Correct the following errors in parallelism:

1. Robert not only forgot to invite two of his fraternity brothers to the wedding but also his banker. ____________________

____

____

2. His father-in-law offered Robert nothing, neither a position with the brokerage firm or a monthly allowance. __________

____

____

3. During the convocation ceremony the spectators smiled both at their friends and relatives or the funny looking Grand Marshal who proudly carried the university banner. __________

____

____

4. The committee abandoned plans for the senior examination because neither the Board of Regents or the system lawyers believed it would prove anything or be worth the trouble.

____

____

As you read for class assignments or pleasure, watch for sentences that follow this pattern and add them below.

PATTERN 16a: MORE PAIRED CONSTRUCTIONS, FOR CONTRAST ONLY

A "this, not that" construction
____ .
in some place other than the verb position

EXPLANATION:

This type of paired construction—the simple contrast—illustrates the differences between two ideas and usually involves a reversal. This simple contrast by reversal may be dramatically emphatic or may simply reenforce an ironic purpose. Unlike PATTERN 16, this one does *not* involve the correlative conjunctions. If you want to show a reversal in the middle of your statement, simply say something is "*this,* not *that*" or "not *this,* but *that.*" Punctuation marks—especially commas, dashes, or parentheses—will help make a break in your sentence and establish your point of reversal or contrast.

EXAMPLES:

By just a quirk of fate (not by deliberate choice) Columbus landed in the Carribean, not the Gulf of Mexico; in the West Indies, not the East Indies.

Money—not love—was the reason the showgirl married the millionaire.

We are not angry; simply disgusted and ready to quit.
(Note the ellipsis and the contrast.)

Justice often imposes a conception on the poor of having problems, not grievances, of needing treatment, not justice.

Chew on ideas, not words.

People's minds are changed through observation, never through argument.

His own actions, not those of his adversaries, are his undoing.

Most students have to learn that "meanings" are in people, not in messages.

The judge asked for acquittal—not conviction.

EXERCISES:

Using the following sentences for words and ideas, construct contrasting "this, not that" sentences. Use dashes and parentheses as well as commas to establish your point of reversal.

1. Saddle-bronc riding is the classic rodeo event even though many spectators prefer the dangerous brahma bullriding contests. ______________________________

____

____

2. Although Jules resembled a skilled ski coach, he was merely a male model displaying a $500 ski ensemble. ______________

____

____

3. With horror Sandra realized that Jerrell was a werewolf; he had been masquerading as a royal prince of Transylvania.

____

____

Create complete sentences using the indicated point of contrast.

1. ______________________________ — not romance — ______________________________ .

2. ________ ________________________ , not freedom .

3. ________________________________ (not just milk and a sandwich) ________________________

________________________________ .

Create a point of contrast for the following incomplete structures.

1. The argument was the result of two clashing philosophies — not ________________________________ .

2. The ballerina could wear the dainty satin slippers , but not

________________________________ .

3. No ________________ _ _ , Rafael ate his dessert with gusto .

4. The voters did not want dissolute politicians , ________

________________________________ .

5. A student wants to know the truth , not merely ________

________________________________ .

As you read for class assignments or pleasure, watch for sentences that follow this pattern and add them below.

____

____

____

PATTERN 17:	DEPENDENT CLAUSES (in a "sentence slot") AS SUBJECT **OR** OBJECT **OR** COMPLEMENT

S [dependent clause as subject] V ____________ .

S V [dependent clause as object or comp.] ____________ .

EXPLANATION:

As you learn to vary your sentence structures, alternating simple with more complex ones, you will find this pattern especially helpful in achieving variety and style. Although a sophisticated pattern, it is (strangely enough) quite common in speech; it is easy to use in your written work, too, if you understand that the dependent clause is merely a part of the independent clause.

The dependent clauses in this pattern, which serve as nouns, will begin with one of the following words

who, whom, which, that, what, why, where, when

after which will come the subject—verb of the dependent clause. If one of these introductory words IS the subject, it will need only a verb after it.

EXAMPLES:

[*How he could fail*] is a mystery to me.
(subject of verb *is*)

He became [*what he had long aspired to be.*]
(complement after *become*)

[*What man cannot imagine,*] he cannot create.
(object of *can create* in this "inverted" sentence)

Juliet never realizes [*why her decision to drink the sleeping potion is irrational.*]
(object of verb *realizes*)

[*Why many highly literate people continue to watch insipid soap operas on television*] constantly amazes writers, producers, even directors.
(subject of *amazes*)

[*That he was a werewolf*] became obvious within a few moments after his fingernails turned into claws.
(subject of verb *became*)

CHECKPOINTS:

✔ Remember that the dependent clause can never stand alone; it is only a portion of your sentence. Therefore don't put a period before or after it because you will create an awkward fragment. For instance, these two examples are wrong:

With horror she realized that he was a philanderer. Confirming her mother's low opinion of him.

Juliet never realizes why her decision to drink the sleeping potion is irrational. Which explains why she drinks it.

How would you correct these errors?

EXERCISES:

Insert a dependent clause in each of the blanks. Be sure each clause has a subject—verb combination.

1. After many years of research the scientist realized that

   ____ .

2. Why ______________________________________ the

   members of the social club will never understand .

3. What swimmers __________________________________

   ________ , they can definitely accomplish .

4. That ____

   became clearer to me as I thought over his answer .

5. How often she ___________________________________

   ________ shocked not only _______________________

_______________ but also _______________________

____ .

As you read for class assignments or pleasure, watch for sentences that follow this pattern and add them below.

____

____

____

____

____

____

____

____

____

____

PATTERN 18: ABSOLUTE CONSTRUCTION ANYWHERE IN SENTENCE
(noun plus participle)

Absolute construction , S V

S , absolute construction , V

OR

— —

OR

( )

EXPLANATION:

What exactly is an absolute construction? It is a noun or pronoun plus a participle with no grammatical connection to the independent clause. What's so absolute about it? Only its absolute independence, its lack of any grammatical connection to the sentence. At home in any part of the sentence, an absolute construction is a separate entity and provides further information without modifying anything. Maybe these constructions are called "absolute" because they are absolutely different from anything else in English grammar; they are not dependent clauses because they have no verbs, and they could never be independent clauses for the same reason.

ABSOLUTE: His blanket being torn, Linus cried on Charlie Brown's shoulder.

DEPENDENT CLAUSE: Because his blanket was torn, Linus cried on Charlie Brown's shoulder.

If carefully used, this pattern will be one of your most helpful devices for varying sentence structure. If tossed into a sentence cavalierly, it may create inexcusable awkwardness. Try not to force this construction but look for places in your paragraph where it would seem natural.

You may work with irregular participles (*torn* and *burnt* here):

His blanket torn and his finger burnt, Linus cried on Charlie Brown's shoulder.

Or you can work with present participles:

The American economy, God willing, will soon return to normal.

His early efforts failing, Teddy tried a new approach to the calculus problem.

If you wish, you may even use several participles and then contradict all of them with a contrasting adjective as the following sentence illustrates:

Caesar continued his march through Gaul, his army tattered, exhausted, hardened—but victorious.

EXAMPLES:

The walls being blank, the new tenant—an unemployed artist—promptly set about covering all of them in a mural of orange, vermillion, and yellow.

I plan to sail to Tahiti (my pension permitting) as soon as I retire from this company.

We had our Memorial Day picnic after all, the rain having stopped before sunset.

The crayons being all used up, Angelo stopped marking on the newly painted table.

All things considered, the situation seems favorable.

What the dog reflects is his master's true emotion, admitted or not.

Faced with overwhelming abundance, the pioneers often killed many more buffalo than they needed for food—the greatest wildlife slaughter the world has ever known.

CHECKPOINTS:

✔ Because it has no grammatical connection with the sentence, the absolute construction must always have some punctuation. Use a comma after an absolute phrase at the first of the sentence or before one at the end. Such a phrase in the middle of the sentence must have a pair of commas or dashes or parentheses.

EXERCISES:

Provide an absolute construction for the blanks in each of the following sentences:

1. The tantalizing aromas from my grandmother's kitchen linger in my memory, all of them ______________________ __________ .
2. The little boy stood beside the swimming pool, his eyes ______________________________________ .
3. Their nostrils ______________________ , the race horses ______________________________ .
4. The sounds of the airport — jets ______________________ ________ , people ______________________ , the public address system ______________________ — suggest the excitement and frustration and chaos of the place
5. The accordion player's hands raced over the keys, his right hand ______________________________ , his left hand ______________________ .

As you read for class assignments or pleasure, watch for sentences that follow this pattern and add them below.

____

PATTERN 19: THE SHORT SIMPLE SENTENCE FOR RELIEF OR DRAMATIC EFFECT

S V ________ .

EXPLANATION:

This pattern for a short sentence can provide intense clarity, but brevity alone will not make it dramatic. Actually, this pattern will be effective only

when you employ it deliberately after several long sentences,

or when you let it more or less summarize what you have just said,

or when you let it provide transition between two or more ideas.

"All was lost" or "Thus it ended" may not look very startling here, but in the appropriate context they might be quite dramatic. After a series of long, involved sentences, a statement with only a few words can arrest your reader's attention, make him pause, shock her into considering the ideas in the longer sentences that precede it. This pattern may, indeed, condense or point up what you have taken several longer sentences to explain.

Developing your style involves practice and training your ear to hear "a good turn of the phrase."

Polonius knew this.

EXAMPLES:

Days passed.

But then it happened.

All efforts failed.

Just consider this.

Well, I wonder.

And this is true.

I think not!

The frontier was open.

And so it was.

"Call me Ishmael." (the dramatic first sentence in *Moby Dick*)

NOTE: Try to imagine the kind of context that would make these sentences dramatic and effective. You might also consider how experienced writers, such as Charles Dickens, manipulate short sentences or join a number of short, balanced thoughts into one long sentence that could have been broken down into a series of short sentences, brief and dramatic. But imagine how choppy the opening of *Tale of Two Cities* would have sounded if Dickens had peppered the first paragraph with short sentences rather than one long sentence, with a series of parallel and balanced parts:

> "It was the best of times, it was the worst of times, it was the age of wisdom, it was the age of foolishness, it was the epoch of belief, it was the epoch of incredulity, it was the season of Light, it was the season of Darkness, it was the spring of hope, it was the winter of despair, we had everything before us, we had nothing before us, we were all going direct to Heaven, we were all going direct the other way—in short, the period was so far like the present period, that some of its noisiest authorities insisted on its being received, for good or for evil, in the superlative degree of comparison only."
>
> —Charles Dickens, *Tale of Two Cities*

CHECKPOINTS:

✔ Length is not the criterion here.

✔ Don't think that sentences such as "I like petunias" or "Children laugh" fit this pattern just because they are short. They might, of course, but only in the proper context.

✔ Look in your reading to discover how professional writers employ this technique of short sentences for special effects.

✔ This pattern is best when it is emphatic, points up a contrast, or summarizes dramatically.

EXERCISES:

As you read for classroom assignments or pleasure, observe how professional writers often use the short simple sentence for dramatic effect. Copy the sentence here and add a comment about its function in the overall context—to provide transition, to give relief, to shock the reader, etc.

1. Example: ____

____

Comment: ____

____

2. Example: ____

____

Comment: ____

____

3. Example: ____

____

Comment: ____

____

4. Example: ____

____

Comment: ____

____

5. Example: ____

____

Comment: ____

____

PATTERN 19a:	A SHORT QUESTION FOR DRAMATIC EFFECT

(Interrogative word) auxiliary verb	S	V	?
(Interrogative word standing alone)			?
(Question based solely on intonation)			?
Auxiliary verb	S	V	?

EXPLANATION:

This pattern has two basic constructions: a question that begins with an interrogative word, or a statement that becomes a question through intonation (pitch or tone) of voice.

It is effective in several places:

in the introduction to arouse the reader's interest;

as a topic sentence to introduce a paragraph;

within the paragraph to provide variety;

between paragraphs to provide transition;

at the end to provide a thought-provoking conclusion.

Look in these five places to discover where a question could serve some desired effect in your writing. Provoke your reader with staccato-like questions, wake him up, make him pause and think, make her ask *why* or *wherefore* about your subject.

EXAMPLES:

What caused the change?

Then why did he?

What comes next?

When will it end?

These examples of questions made with intonation are more common in conversation than in formal prose:

That's her mother?

You made an A in Esch's class?

James flunked modern dance?

CHECKPOINTS:

✔ Questions need to be handled carefully to be effective.

✔ Avoid scattering them around just because they are easy; make them serve some purpose, such as to arouse curiosity, to stimulate interest, to lead the reader into some specific idea about your subject.

EXERCISES:

In whatever you might be reading look for the short dramatic question. Copy the sentence here and add a comment about its function within the overall context; recall that there are at least five effects.

1. Example: ______________________________

____

Comment: ______________________________

____

2. Example: ______________________________

____

Comment: ______________________________

____

3. Example: ______________________________

____

Comment: ______________________________

____

4. Example: ______________________________

____

Comment: ______________________________

____

5. Example: ______________________________

____

Comment: ______________________________

____

PATTERN 20: THE DELIBERATE FRAGMENT

Merely a part of a sentence

EXPLANATION:

The mere mention of the word "fragment" chills the blood of some overly traditional teachers; but a master stylist, ironically enough, often relies on brief sentence fragments to give emphasis and a sense of immediacy to his or her prose. This deliberate fragment should create a dramatic effect within a paragraph; it should serve some purpose, such as forcing the reader to look backward. If it doesn't, don't use it. It would not be appropriate. Often only the context in which the fragment appears can tell whether to put it in or leave it out. Used sparingly, the fragment can be as effective as the rhetorical question or the short dramatic sentence. Used injudiciously, it is simply another ineffective gimmick.

EXAMPLES:

Try a fragment

- in a description—

  I wish you could have known the Southwest in the early days. The way it really was. The way the land seemed to reach out forever. And those endless blue stretches of sky! The incredible clarity of air which made distance an illusion. I wish I could make you see it so you would understand my nostalgia, nostalgia and sorrow for a wonder that is no more.

- for transition—

  Now, on with the story.

  But to get back to the subject.

  So much for that.

  Next? The crucial question to be answered.

- in structuring a question or an answer—

  But how?

What then? Nothing.

Based on logic? Hardly!

Where and when and why?

Upon what does wisdom finally depend? Primarily upon the ability to know and understand—to see through sham.

- for making exclamations and for emphasis—

What a price to pay!

All these achievements before his twenty-third birthday!

The next step—martyrdom.

There is a price to fame. The agonizing price of self-denial, the price of blood and sweat and tears.

Oh, the many problems the lobsterman faces, notwithstanding the scarcity of lobsters!

- and sometimes in aphorisms or fragments of clichés—

The more the merrier for them, too.

Early to bed!

A bird in the hand, old buddy. Remember?

Absolute power corrupting once more.

CHECKPOINTS:

✔ If you are in the habit of writing fragmentary sentences, don't think that you have already mastered this pattern!

✔ Like PATTERNS 19 and 19a, this one must be a deliberate styling device. It can never be merely an accident or a mistake in sentence structure or punctuation.

CAUTION: Use PATTERNS 19, 19a, and 20 sparingly and precisely.

EXERCISES:

In your reading look for highly styled, deliberate fragments used for dramatic effect. Copy the fragment and add a brief comment about its function or purpose.

1. Example: ______________________________

____

Comment: ______________________________

____

2. Example: ______________________________

____

Comment: ______________________________

____

3. Example: ______________________________

____

Comment: ______________________________

____

4. Example: ______________________________

____

Comment: ______________________________

____

5. Example: ______________________________

____

Comment: ______________________________

____

CHAPTER 3

SENTENCES GROW SOME MORE

NOW you are ready to make sentences grow . . . and grow some more.

Now that you are familiar with some of the more complex patterns in CHAPTER 2, let's combine two or more of them to create additional variety in your sentences. Only a few examples of sentence combinations appear in this chapter, but you will discover many more possibilities as you experiment on your own, still remembering these cautions: always try to write a sentence that fits into the total context; never force a construction simply for the sake of variety.

Don't be afraid to be creative. Experiment not only with your own favorite patterns from CHAPTER 2 but also with others, with new ones you will discover in your reading or create in your own writing. When you learn to maneuver sentence patterns, when you feel at ease manipulating words, then you will be a master of sentence structure if not yet a master stylist.

Now to discover what patterns combine well—

Combining the patterns—ten ways

1. The compound sentence with a colon combines effectively with a series and the repetition of a key term (PATTERNS 3, 4, 9a).

To the Victorians much in life was sacred: marriage was sacred, the family circle was sacred, society was sacred, the British empire was sacred.

2. Repetition also combines well with a dependent clause as the interrupting modifier (PATTERNS 9, 11).

The experiences of the past—because they are experiences of the past—too seldom guide our actions today.

3. A dependent clause as complement combines well with an appositive at the end of a sentence after a colon and a series with balanced pairs (PATTERNS 17, 10, 5).

Ted became what he had long aspired to be: a master of magic and illusion, of hypnotism and sleight-of-hand tricks.

4. The series without a conjunction and the repetition of a key term combine well with the introductory appositive and an inversion of any kind (PATTERNS 4, 9, 9a, 15a).

The generation which was too young to remember a depression, too young to remember World War II, too young even to vote—from that generation came America's soldiers for Southeast Asia.

5. The compound sentence without a conjunction can combine with repetitions and series (PATTERNS 1, 4, 4a, 9).

Books of elegiac poetry had always stirred Jason; they made him think of music, music that sang of ancient glories, of brave men, of the things they loved and hated and died for.

6. Introductory appositives may be written as dependent clauses, with one of the clauses having a modifier out of place for emphasis, and the repetition of a key term followed by a question for dramatic effect (PATTERNS 6, 8, 9, 13, 19a).

That there are too many people, that overcrowding causes social, economic, and political problems, that human fellowship and compassion wear thin in such an environment—these are problems facing the inner city today, problems that eventually young people must solve. But how will they?

7. An inversion of the sentence pattern may also include a prepositional phrase before the subject—verb combination within a compound sentence (PATTERNS 1, 14, 15a).

   Around Jay were men of various nationalities; with none of them could he ever really relate.

8. A pair of dependent clauses as direct objects will work well with paired words, a series without a conjunction, an interrupting modifier with dashes, and a repetition of the same word in a parallel construction (PATTERNS 4, 11, 9a, 16, 17).

   The ambassador found that not only was America experiencing painful expansion and costly social upheavals—over foreign policy, racial disorder, economic priorities—but also that the nation was facing the threat of a national paralysis of will, a paralysis of faith.

9. An interrupting modifier that is itself a sentence may go well with another type of modifier (PATTERNS 11, 11a).

   His family, a respected conservative family ruled mainly by several maiden aunts—his father had died when he was a child—had been scandalized at the thought that their young heir wanted to devote his entire life to hot-rod racing and roller-derby competition.

10. After a long involved compound sentence without a conjunction, a fragment with a repeated key word and then a fragmentary question may be very effective (PATTERNS 1, 4a, 9a, 20).

    The ecology-awareness movement aims at balance and wholeness and health in our environment; it wants to assure a proper place in the scheme of things for people, for plants, and for animals. Not an exclusive place for either one, just a proper place for all. But how?

Expanding sentences

Frequently writers find that a simple sentence with a single subject and a single verb is too brief or lean, that the meaning is not complete or as clear as it should be. What is missing is a modifier that will add explanations, descriptions, specific details, amplifications, supporting materials to make the sentence clear and meaningful to the reader. Thus, in order to make the point clear, the writer *adds* to the sentence. Modifiers help the reader visualize and illustrate the generalization expressed in the basic sentence. These modifiers may be words, phrases, clauses that appear at the beginning, the middle, or the end of the sentence; they may also modify one another.

Think of the basic idea, the primary kernel sentence, as the first level of writing and the modifiers added for clarity as the second or the third or the fourth level of writing. Each successive level is related to the one immediately above it and is related to the basic sentence by the intervening modifiers, some subordinating, some coordinating. Later on, as you acquire more experience in writing, look for a generalization or an abstract word in your sentence—clear to you but possibly not to your reader—that will require you to shift and backtrack, adding modifiers at different levels to help the reader comprehend fully the meaning you have in mind. Francis Christensen, *Notes Toward a New Rhetoric* (New York: Harper and Row, 1967) named this type of expanded sentence the "cumulative sentence." In it the base sentence of main subject and main verb with their "bound modifiers" (those that cannot move about) *accumulates* additions. To the base one adds "free modifiers" (those that can move about) that enrich the sentence and create a feeling of motion. A more recent description of the Christensen method appears in *A New Rhetoric* (New York: Harper and Row, 1976).

Study the examples below and notice how modifiers on different levels in the subject slot here help expand the sentence and clarify its meaning.

LEVEL ONE: the basic slots for any sentence (S—V)

Whooping cranes fly. (the "kernel sentence," according to Francis Christensen)

Now, on different levels add modifiers to the subject.

LEVEL TWO (the first modifiers): may come before or after subject:

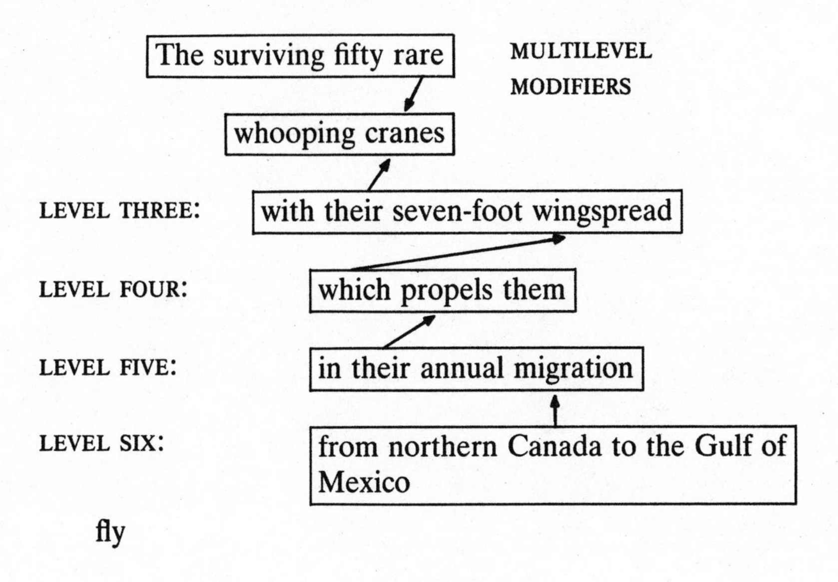

unerringly.

Now add more modifiers on different levels in the verb slot:

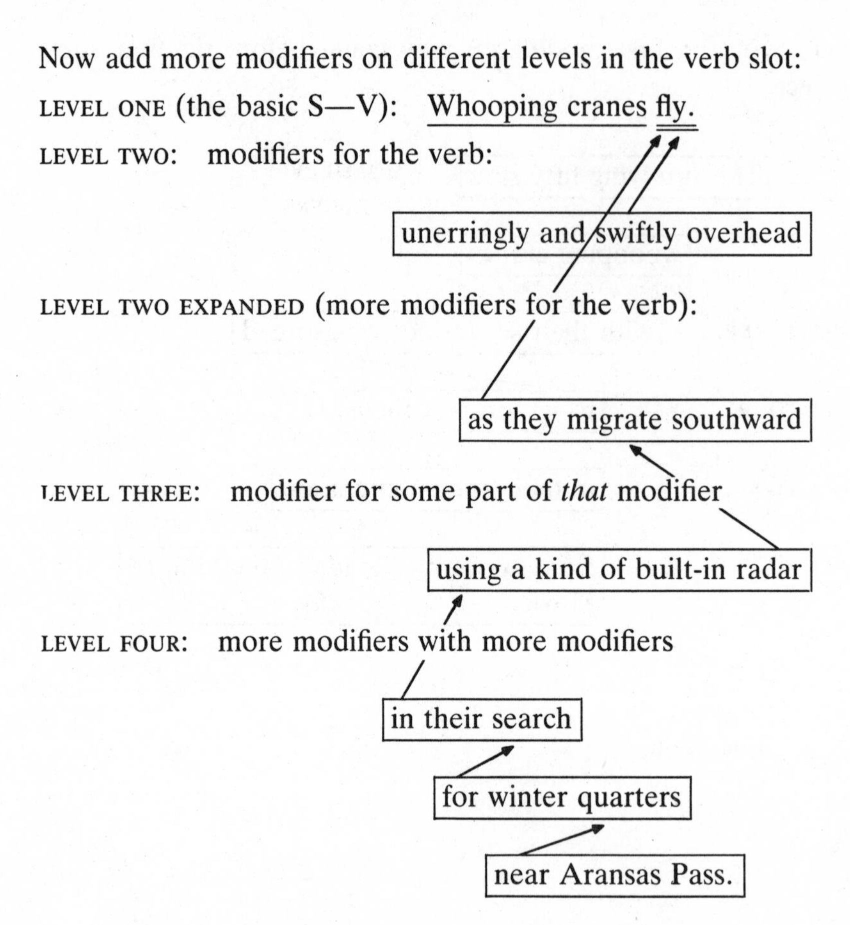

Now see what modifiers can do to a basic sentence:

> The surviving fifty rare whooping cranes, with their seven-foot wingspread which propels them in their annual migration from northern Canada to the Gulf of Mexico, fly unerringly and swiftly overhead as they migrate southward using a kind of built-in radar in their search for winter quarters near Aransas Pass.

CHAPTER 4

FIGURATIVE LANGUAGE IN SENTENCES

Spice up your sentences with some interesting and original figures of speech. These are the fresh, picture-making phrases that say one thing but mean something different or something more.

Figurative language helps words say more and mean more than their actual, literal meanings convey. It demands from the reader an understanding of the many connotations a word may have, an ability to picture or realize the image behind the figure of speech. It also demands something from the writer: avoiding the colorless cliché. Once you understand what the various figures of speech are, once you master their "patterns," you will have no trouble thinking up original ones of your own.

Figures of speech

SIMILE: A simile is a stated comparison between essentially unalike things, things from different classes. You must have one of the following connectives in all similes: *like, as, than,* or a verb such as *seems.* A simile says that two things are similar when they are not really alike at all.

EXAMPLES: Trying to pin a reason on the sudden elopement of those two is a little like trying to nail Jello to the wall.

It's about as easy as striking a match on a mirror.

Since 1945, the threat of total annihilation has roosted, like a vulture in a tree, in Western Man's awareness.

Betsy's first soufflé looked flatter than a punctured balloon.

Casanova found his mistresses' eyes were nothing like the sun. (This simile also makes an *allusion* to Shakespeare's Sonnet CXXX.)

METAPHOR: A metaphor is an implied comparison. It is implied because you do not say that something is "like" or "as" another thing; you simply say that one thing IS something else. (A is B.) As with similes, here again, the two things being compared must be unlike things from different classes.

There are two types of metaphors.

TYPE 1: The "A equals B" type uses two terms.

The sky is a blue tapestry.

The dragonfly is a blue thread hovering over the pool.

TYPE 2: The single-word metaphor can imply or suggest a comparison.

a. *verbs:* Almost any sports page will yield a rich harvest of these verbs with picture-making power.

The young rookie of the Milwaukee Bucks skyrocketed to fame.

The quarterback blasted through the line of Nebraska's defense.

The fans came unglued and jumped up in a frenzy of excitement.

Dr. J operated on his opponents in the NBA finals.

b. *nouns:* The image or picture of comparison comes implied in a noun, which names one thing by calling it another; for example, see the word "harvest" in the preceding sentence explaining *verbs.*

The Arkansas defense line-up was a brick wall—impenetrable and invulnerable.

The quarterback crossed the line into the Promised Land, giving Ohio State six more points and a Rose Bowl win.

Harvard freshmen often think there should be an easier ascent up Parnassus than the one prescribed in the university catalogue.

c. *adjectives:* Adjectives may also imply comparisons; they describe something in terms that no reader would ever take literally.

Cynthia's feline movements clawed into Harold's composure. (Here, both "feline" and "clawed" are metaphors, suggesting something cat-like about Cynthia.)

"Every slaughtered syllable is a kindness to your reader," declared the lecturer addressing the budding young journalists.

CHECKPOINTS: Don't "mix" your images in a metaphor. Look at these ghastly creations!

They stepped forth into the sea of matrimony and found it a very rocky road.

The "ship of state" might be off its keel; it might sink or flounder or get off course without a firm hand at the helm, but it could never bog down in a storm of red tape or be the leader of the team or surge ahead in second gear.

ANALOGY: An analogy is really only an extended metaphor or simile. Analogy is an attempt to compare at length two objects from different classes; a classic analogy compares the human heart to a mechanical pump, for example, or the eye to a camera. This type of comparison carried to its extreme conclusion will, of course, be illogical because in no analogy will the various parts of the two unlike objects be completely comparable.

Analogy, however, does help you to clarify some comparison you are trying to make; if appropriate and not far-fetched, it will help you to sustain a clarifying comparison throughout a short paragraph or even a long, extended piece of prose. Analogies should help you to enrich your writing, to interpret some meaning or significance about your main points, to reflect your particular way of thinking about things, to add wit and charm to your style.

EXAMPLE: The New York Public Library might hold the key to your future; it unlocks many doors to knowledge; it opens the way to numerous opportunities. (This would be merely metaphor unless you extended it a little further.)

The human brain in some ways resembles a computer. (Now, go on—complete the analogy by showing how.)

Life is like the movies: there are so many kinds of plots, but you should be the director of your own script. (Does this suggest how you might discuss life as tragedy, comedy, melodrama, adventure?)

To the new student the college campus is like a forest—all trees, each indistinguishable from the other and each an obstacle in his or her path. (Extend this analogy by describing how the student finds the way through the "forest" and comes to know the name—and function—of each "tree.")

CHECKPOINT: Never rely on an analogy as proof in logic or argument. An analogy is simply an imaginative comparison of two completely different things.

ALLUSION: Allusion is another way of making comparison; it suggests a similarity between what you are writing about and something that your reader has read before or heard about. The success of the allusion, of course, will depend on whether you strike a responsive chord in your reader's memory.

Allusions, richly connotative or symbolic, always suggest more than the words say. Because they are rich with overtones, your writing benefits by conjuring up for your readers all they remember from their past.

If you want to allude to something, let a word, phrase, or even your very style suggest a similarity between the subject and some other idea, a similarity real or imaginary. Success with allusions depends in part on your readers; after all, they must be able to recognize what you are alluding to. So choose allusions that will fit your audience as well as the context of your paper.

Remember that obscure allusions will cloud communication, but that appropriate ones will enable you to say more in fewer words. Try to use fresh allusions, for stale ones that have become clichés will merely bore your reader.

Common referents are history, the Bible, mythology, literature, popular personalities. In fact, a whole group of words entered the language first as allusions to celebrities and entertainers: a political maverick, a boycott, sandwiches, the little corsican, a Mae West life jacket, an Achilles heel. How many allusions can you find in popular advertising? Or in book titles? Or in popular music?

Grapes of Wrath and *East of Eden* (both allude to the Bible)
Tender Is the Night (alludes to Keats' nightingale ode)
The Sun Also Rises (alludes to Ecclesiastes)
Leave Her to Heaven (alludes to *Hamlet*)
Wonderland (alludes to *Alice in Wonderland*)

These book titles have allusions; can you add other titles to the list?

EXAMPLES: Even if you have miles to go, you should never abandon a project without finishing it.
(alludes to Robert Frost's "The Road Not Taken")

Deciding that a man's reach must exceed his grasp, Charlie decided to continue trying for top billing on the marquee.
(alludes to Robert Browning's "Andrea del Sarto")

Flee now; pray later. (In style, this should remind the reader of the familiar "Fly now; pay later" advertising slogan.)

The omnipresent ticking of the clock on the wall made him feel chained to time.
(alludes to Shelley's "Adonais")

The 1980 United States team at the Winter Olympics became the Cinderella team of international hockey competition.

IRONY: Perhaps the most useful figurative device from poetry and oral delivery is *irony*—the concealing of intended meaning in words that convey the opposite meaning. Ironic language presents a discrepancy between what is real and what is intended. You have heard compliments, which were actually veiled criticism; the tone of a speaker's delivery conveys the real meaning. Try pronouncing "He's no fool," conveying different meanings with the same words. Ironical remarks are softer than the harsher, sarcastic speech. In sarcasm both speaker and listener know the real meaning of the message, whereas in irony meaning is subtler and less biting.

In prose, irony can be a powerful weapon. Jonathan Swift expertly attacked the Irish Catholics in his ironical *A Modest Proposal* by presenting a wholly unacceptable answer to overpopulation in logic so ironic that Swift's readers, while outraged, found themselves succumbing to his closing ironical statements: "I profess in the sincerity of my heart that I have not the least personal interest in endeavoring to promote this necessary work, having no other good than the public good of my country, by advancing our trade, providing for infants, relieving the poor, and giving some pleasure to the rich. I have no children by which I can propose to get a single penny; the youngest being nine years old, and my wife past child-bearing."

HYPERBOLE AND UNDERSTATEMENT: In prose, two special types of irony—also apparent in poetry—are useful in communicating a message effectively: *hyperbole* (overstatement) and *understatement* (litotes). A bold, deliberately exaggerated statement is hyperbolic. The statement is an exaggeration that stresses the truth, but one does not expect the statement to be believed. Ironic in context, hyperbole can produce a fanciful effect or something comic or absurd. The speaker in Andrew Marvell's "To His Coy Mistress" uses hyperbole to present a good line to his beloved, suggesting that if they had all the time in the world he would adore her patiently and lavishly: "An hundred years should go to praise / Thine eyes, and on thy forehead gaze; / Two hundred to adore each breast, / But thirty thousand to the rest." Try adding a hyperbolic one-liner to add humor to your message. Of a sudden thunder shower, you might write, "Wonderful day, isn't it?" Or in describing a large cocktail party, you might try to impress your audience by recalling, "There were millions of people there, at least two hundred of my dearest, closest friends!"

By contrast, understatement deliberately says *less* than what is actually intended. The speaker or writer offers us the message by stating the negative or opposite. From this seeming contradiction comes an emphatic statement that is the heart of the message. Saying of a very wise man "He's no fool" helps stress the man's intelligence through the understated message. You might write an elaborate description of a fine meal, then underplay the excellence by saying "not bad." Listen how Christopher Johns underplays the horror of a drink in which a poisonous snake floats: "A raw fish meal is called sashimi, and the ideal accompaniment to it is considered to be some double-distilled sake in the bottling of which a live Marmushi has been added. A Marmushi is a poisonous snake. I will spare the reader further details."*

*Christopher Johns, "Ah So!" *The Journal of the International Wine and Food Society*, 6, No. 3 (February 1980), p. 30.

Further reading

If you need additional information or more complete descriptions of figurative language in poetry and prose, you might wish to consult one of the following standard reference works:

Barnet, Sylvan, Morton Berman, and William Burto. *A Dictionary of Literary, Dramatic, and Cinematic Terms,* 2nd ed. Boston: Little, Brown, and Company, 1971.

Fowler, H. W. *A Dictionary of Modern English Usage,* 2nd ed. New York: Oxford University Press, 1965.

Holman, C. Hugh. *A Handbook to Literature,* 4th ed. Indianapolis: Bobbs-Merrill Educational Publishing, 1980.

Preminger, Alex, ed. *Encyclopedia of Poetry and Poetics.* Princeton: Princeton University Press, 1965.

CHAPTER 5

THE TWENTY PATTERNS— IN PRINT

TOUGH COUNTRY*

—from *Tularosa* by C. L. Sonnichsen

	SENTENCE PATTERNS
The Tularosa country is a parched desert where everything, from cactus to cowman, carries a weapon of some sort, and the only creatures who sleep with both eyes closed are dead.	11
In all the sun-scorched and sand-blasted reaches of the Southwest there is no grimmer region. Only the fierce and the rugged can live here—prickly pear and mesquite; rattlesnake and tarantula. True, Texas cattlemen made the cow a native of the region seventy-five years ago, but she would have voted against the step if she had been asked.	14 10a 5
From the beginning this lonesome valley has been a laboratory for developing endurance, a stern school specializing in just one subject: the Science of Doing Without.	14 10
Everything has been done to promote the success of the experiments. There is almost no water; no shade. High mountain walls all around keep out the tenderfeet. On the west, screening off the Rio Grande valley with its green fields and busy highways, great ridges of limestone and granite—Franklin and Organ; San Andres and Oscuro—heave and roll northward from El Paso. Across the valley to the eastward, shutting off the oases along the Pecos, the	9a 14 12 5 and 7 14

SENTENCE PATTERNS

Hueco mountains merge with the pine-cloaked Sacramentos, and these give way to Sierra Blanca and Jicarilla, with 12,000-foot Sierra Blanca Peak soaring in naked majesty over all.

12

The Tularosa country lies between the ranges, a great pocket of sand, sun, and sparse vegetation thirty miles wide, more or less, and over two hundred miles long. The Jumanos Mesa, named for a long-vanished tribe of Indians, gives it a northern boundary. To the south it merges with the Chihuahua Desert which pushes far down into Mexico.

11
11

Seen from the tops of the screening ranges, it looks like a flat, gray-green, sun-flooded expanse of nothing, impressive only because the eye can travel a hundred miles and more in one leap. Near at hand it is full of surprises. The northern end of the valley is a little less parched. Grass still grows tall on Carrizozo Flat, and bean farmers have plowed up the country around Claunch. Nearby, two prehistoric lava flows cover the land with an appalling jumble of volcanic rock known locally as the *malpais.*

14
12
4
13

South of the lava flows, the vast gypsum deposits called the White Sands spread out in a deathly, glittering world of pure white which edges eastward a few inches every year, threatening in a few millennia to swallow up everything as far as the Sacramentos.

12

Sometimes the valley floor heaves in sand dunes; sometimes it breaks into red hummocks, each one crowned with the delicate green leaves and lethal thorns of a mesquite bush. There are broad swales where the yuccas grow in groves—leprous alkali flats where even the sturdy greasewood can barely hold its own—long inclines of tall grama grass where the foothills rise to the knees of the mountains—and

1
9a 18

countless acres of prickly pear and *lechuguilla* and rabbit brush.

A harsh, forbidding country, appalling to newcomers from gentler regions. But it has its moments of intense beauty. Sunrise and sunset are magic times. Under a full moon, that lonely, whispering waste is transformed into an austere corner of fairyland. The belated traveler catches his breath when the tender fingers of dawn pick out the tiny black shapes of the pine trees far above him on the top of the Sacramentos. One does not forget the Organs blackening against the sunset, swathed in a veil of lilac shadows—the eerie gleam of the white sands at moonrise—a swarthy cloud dissolving in a column of rain, the froth of impact showing white at its foot while all round the sun shines serenely on.

The yucca is a thorny and cantankerous object, but in the spring it puts up a ten-foot stalk which explodes in a mass of creamy-white blossoms. And so it is with other sullen citizens of the desert when their time comes: the prickly pear with its rich yellow flower, the desert willow dripping with pendent pink and lavender, little pincushion cacti robing themselves in mauve petals more gorgeous than roses, the ocotillo shrouding its savage spines in tiny green leaves till its snaky arms look like wands of green fur, each one tipped with a long finger of pure scarlet.

It is big country—clean country—and if it has no tenderness, it has strength and a sort of magnificence.

To live there has always been a risky business—a matter not only of long chances and short shrifts but also of privation and danger. This was true of the prehistoric cave dwellers who lived only a little better than their animal neighbors in the Huecos many

SENTENCE PATTERNS

4a

20
19

14

12
4 (with dashes)
12
18

10

4

18

9
16a

16 and 5
(Note repetition of "true" in parallel construction here)

SENTENCE PATTERNS

centuries gone by. It was true of the little pueblo communities which grew up later in the mountain canyons and wherever a wet-weather lake made existence possible on the valley floor. It was true in historic times of the peaceful Christian Indians who abandoned their unfinished church at Gran Quivira when the Apaches overwhelmed them nearly three hundred years ago.

Yes, it has always been hard country—frontier country—and for obvious reasons, the first reason being those same Apaches. The slopes of the Sierra Blanca were their favorite haunts as far back as we have any records, and though they ranged far and wide over the desert and even moved to Mexico for decades when the Comanches descended upon them, they always came back to the mountain rivers and the tall pines. A merciless environment made them tough and almost unbeatable fighters. They kept their country to themselves as long as they were able, waging a never-ending war against hunger and thirst, Comanches and Mexicans, soldiers and settlers, until their power was broken less than a lifetime ago.

9
9 and 18
12 and 5

Highways and railroads were slow in coming to a region so far removed from the gathering places of men and money. Sheer isolation did what the Apache was not able to do alone: it held off the traders and developers for years while the Rio Grande and Pecos settlements were booming.

17
3

But the most potent force of all for keeping people out was plain, old-fashioned, skin-cracking drought. The rainfall was imperceptible, and there was just enough ground water available to cause trouble. On the valley floor there was next to none at all until men got around to drilling wells. A few springs existed here and there in the Organs and the

4
14

SENTENCE PATTERNS

San Andres, none of them big enough to supply more than a few men and beasts. The eastern mountains were higher and better supplied. Spring-fed streams came down from the Sierra Blanca at Three Rivers, while Tularosa Creek descended the pass between Sierra Blanca and Sacramento beside the main trail from the Pecos to the Rio Grande.

Farther south, where the mile-high cliffs of the Sacramentos soar above the plain, a number of canyons drained off the water from the heights—Dog Canyon and Agua Chiquita; Sacramento and Grapevine. In Sacramento Canyon and in Dog Canyon the water was more or less permanent. But everywhere, until the skill and cupidity of man turned the liquid gold to account, it flowed out onto the flats a pitifully short distance and disappeared in the sand. Along with it, as the years passed, flowed the blood of many a man who gave up his life for a trickle of water.

13
10a
5
14
13
15a

Sensible men, cautious men, stayed away from such a place. But the adventurous and the hardy and the reckless kept on coming. Each one had a dream of some sort—water for his cows, solitude for his soul, gold to make him rich. For even the Tularosa country has its treasures. The ghostly ruins of Gran Quivira have been honeycombed by men obsessed with the notion that the Indians buried a hoard of gold before they left. At the northeast corner of the valley, in the Jicarilla Mountains, lies the abandoned gold camp of White Oaks, the site of rich mining properties seventy years ago. Midway between El Paso and Alamogordo, on the rocky slopes of the Jarillas, Orogrande sits solitary, remembering the days when prospectors and miners swarmed in; and a few miles away at the San Augustin Pass the abandoned shafts at Organ tell a similar tale.

9a
4a
4
14
15a
12

But the real story of Tularosa is the story of Texas cattlemen—drifting herdsmen who began to invade the valley in the early eighties, bringing their stern folkways with them. They too ran into trouble, for their law was not the law of the Mexicans or the Indians or the Yankees who arrived during and after the Civil War. It was those proud riders who kept the Old West alive in that lonely land until yesterday. It was the clash of their ways and standards with the ways and standards of the settled citizens which caused the feuds and killings and hatreds that make up the unwritten history of the region. The Apaches and the climate and the lay of the land helped. But in the last analysis it was the Texans who made Tularosa the Last of the Frontier West.

Those times seem as remote from present-day reality as the wars of Caesar and Charlemagne, but they have left a brand on the soul of many a man and woman still living. That is why this story has never been fully told—why all of it can never be told. For out here in the desert the West of the old days has never quite given way to a newer America. Customs have changed, but attitudes have held fast. To test this fact, try asking questions about certain people and events. Old men clam up and change the subject. Young ones who have heard something hesitate a long time before telling what they know about the sins and tribulations of their grandfathers. Once it was dangerous to talk about these things. Even now it is not considered wise. The fears and loyalties and customs of yesterday—these things still cast their shadows on us who live on the edge of the desert. On the streets of El Paso or Las Cruces or Alamogordo you can still hear the click of bootheels belonging to men who played their parts in dramas which would make a Hollywood movie look tame. Their sons and

SENTENCE PATTERNS

10a
12
4a
Note parallel "it was" construction
9
4a
4a
17
9a
19
19
6
14 and 4a

SENTENCE PATTERNS

daughters still live among us—fine people, too—and their friends still frown on loose discussion. 7a

For these reasons this is not an easy story to tell, but it is time someone told it. So let's go back to the beginning, before the Texas cattle crowded in, ate the grass down to the roots, and trampled the plain into dust—back to the days when the country was the way God made it: bunch grass growing up to a horse's belly; miles of yellow flowers in the wet years; little rainwater lakes at the foot of the Organs and the San Andres, long since dried out and buried in dust; sun and sand and sixty long miles to town. 14 9 4 12 4a

*Reprinted by permission of The Devin-Adair Company.

EXCERPT FROM *A THOUSAND DAYS**

Arthur M. Schlesinger, Jr.

SENTENCE PATTERNS

After Kennedy's death, Adlai Stevenson called him the "contemporary man." His youth, his vitality, his profound modernity—these were final elements in his power and potentiality as he stood on the brink of the Presidency. For Kennedy was not only the first President to be born in the twentieth century. More than that, he was the first representative in the White House of a distinctive generation, the generation which was born during the First World War, came of age during the depression, fought in the Second World War and began its public career in the atomic age.

14
4 and 9a
6
9

This was the first generation to grow up as the age of American innocence was coming to an end. To have been born nearly a decade earlier, like Lyndon Johnson, or nearly two decades earlier, like Adlai Stevenson, was to be rooted in another and simpler America. Scott Fitzgerald had written that his contemporaries grew up "to find all Gods dead, all wars fought, all faiths in man shaken." But the generation which came back from the Second World War found that gods, wars, and faiths in man had, after all, survived if in queer and somber ways. The realities of the twentieth century which had shocked their fathers now wove the fabric of their own lives. Instead of reveling in being a lost generation, they set out in one mood or another to find, if not themselves, a still point in the turning world. The predicament was even worse for the generation which had been too young to fight in the war, too young to recall the age of innocence, the generation which had experienced nothing but turbulence. So in the fifties some sought security at the expense of identity and

11
11
9a
4
14
9a
9
Note parallel construction

SENTENCE PATTERNS

became organization men. Others sought identity at the expense of security and became beatniks. Each course created only a partial man. There was need for a way of life, a way of autonomy, between past and present, the organization man and the anarchist, the square and the beat.

19
9
5

It was autonomy which this humane and self-sufficient man seemed to embody. Kennedy simply could not be reduced to the usual complex of sociological generalizations. He was Irish, Catholic, New England, Harvard, Navy, Palm Beach, Democrat and so on; but no classification contained him. He had wrought an individuality which carried him beyond the definitions of class and race, region and religion. He was a free man, not just in the sense of the cold-war cliché, but in the sense that he was, as much as man can be, self-determined and not the servant of forces outside him.

5
16

This sense of wholeness and freedom gave him an extraordinary appeal not only to his own generation but even more to those who came after, the children of turbulence. Recent history had washed away the easy consolations and the old formulas. Only a few things remained on which contemporary man could rely, and most were part of himself—family, friendship, courage, reason, jokes, power, patriotism. Kennedy demonstrated the possibility of the new self-reliance. As he had liberated himself from the past, so he had liberated himself from the need to rebel against the past. He could insist on standards, admire physical courage, attend his church, love his father while disagreeing with him, love his country without self-doubt or self-consciousness. Yet, while absorbing so much of the traditional code, his sensibility was acutely contemporaneous. He voiced the

16
10a
4
16
4 (verbs in series)

SENTENCE PATTERNS

disquietude of the postwar generation—the mistrust of rhetoric, the disdain for pomposity, the impatience with the postures and pieties of other days, the resignation to disappointment. And he also voiced the new generation's longings—for fulfillment in experience, for the subordination of selfish impulses to higher ideals, for a link between past and future, for adventure and valor and honor. What was forbidden were poses, histrionics, the heart on the sleeve and the tongue on the cliché. What was required was a tough, nonchalant acceptance of the harsh present and an open mind toward the unknown future.

This was Kennedy, with his deflationary wartime understatement (when asked how he became a hero, he said, "It was involuntary. They sank my boat"); his contempt for demagoguery (once during the campaign, after Kennedy had disappointed a Texas crowd by his New England restraint, Bill Attwood suggested that next time he wave his arms in the air like other politicians; Kennedy shook his head and wrote—he was saving his voice—"I always swore one thing I'd never do is—" and drew a picture of a man waving his arms in the air); his freedom from dogma, his appetite for responsibility, his instinct for novelty, his awareness and irony and control; his imperturbable sureness in his own powers, not because he considered himself infallible, but because, given the fallibility of all men, he supposed he could do the job as well as anyone else; his love of America and pride in its traditions and ideals.

10a
4
4a
parallel construction with pattern 17
19
1
4 and 4a
16

Why Punctuate?

Long association with the printed page has made most readers expect certain signals to conform to standard conventions.

denrael evah lla dluoc eW
sdrawkcab sdrow daer ot
tes dah sretnirp ylrae fi
yaw taht epyt rieht
and most people find that reading
upside-down is really no trick at all.

Also, we know the shapes of printed words so well that
we can read almost anything when only the tops of letters show
but we have more difficulty when we can see only the bottoms.

The same kind of training has made us come to expect that printed words today will have spaces between them even though in many early writings allthewordsrantogetherwithoutspacesanywherenotevenbet-weensentencesandtherewerenosuchthingsasparagraphs.

In the same way, we have come to expect that punctuation will follow conventions just as we expect to read from left to right and to find spaces between words so do we also expect the marks of punctuation to signal to us something about the relationships of words to each other after all the same arrangement of words for example Joe said Henry is a dirty slob can have two different meanings depending on the punctuation even a few marks to signal the end of each sentence would have helped you in this paragraph to help your reader give him some of the conventional signals we call punctuation marks.

Punctuation: a signal system

In the American English sentence, punctuation functions as a code, a set of signal systems for the reader to which he will respond. If your code is clear, the reader will get your signals. If your code is faulty, the reader will be confused and you will have failed to communicate. Some marks guide the eye; others, the ear. That is, they indicate the intonation

---

Format for this page was partly suggested by John Spradley's article—"The Agenwit of Inpoint"—in JETT (*Journal of English Teaching Techniques*), Spring, 1971, pages 23–31.

(pause, stress, pitch) the reader should use mentally. For instance, the period indicates a full stop with pitch of voice dropped to indicate a long pause, whereas exclamation points "shout" at the reader and indicate he must raise his voice. The period indicates a long pause, whereas the comma indicates a short one. The semicolon signals not only a stop but also "equality": something equally structured will follow. The colon signals that the thought is not complete, that something explanatory will follow: an important word, phrase, sentence, or a formal listing. The colon is a very formal mark, whereas the dash is less formal, and material within parentheses just "whispers" to the reader. Generally speaking, these marks are not interchangeable; each mark has its own function to perform. It is important, therefore, that you learn when to use the following punctuation marks:

COLON:

1. to introduce enumerations after a complete statement
2. before an independent clause which restates in different form the idea of the preceding independent clause (in a compound sentence)
3. to indicate something is to follow, after the words "following," "as follows," or "thus"
4. before a climactic appositive at end of sentence

SEMICOLON:

1. between the independent clauses in a compound sentence without a conjunction
2. between the independent clauses in a compound sentence with a conjunction when there are commas in one or both clauses
3. before transitional connectives (conjunctive adverbs) separating two independent clauses (*however, therefore, furthermore, thus, hence, likewise, moreover, nonetheless, nevertheless*)
4. to separate elements in a series containing internal commas

COMMAS: to separate main sentence elements

1. independent clauses joined by coordinate conjunctions (*and, but, for, or, nor, so, yet*)
2. elements in a series
3. contrasted elements in a *this, not that* construction
4. direct quotation from such constructions as *He said, She answered,* etc.
5. elements in dates, addresses, place names
6. long introductory phrase or an adverbial clause preceding the main clause
7. an inverted element
8. any elements that might be misread or which might otherwise seem to run together
9. important omissions, elliptical constructions
10. absolute constructions at the beginning or the end of a sentence

COMMAS: a pair to enclose

1. any interrupting construction between subject and verb, verb and object or complement, or any two elements not normally separated
2. an appositive
3. nouns or pronouns of direct address
4. non-restrictive (*not* essential) interrupting modifiers
5. absolute constructions within sentences
6. any parenthetical expression within sentences

DASH: to separate sentence elements

1. before a summary word to separate an introductory series of appositives from the independent clause
2. before an emphatic appositive at the end of a sentence
3. occasionally before a repetition for emphasis

DASHES: a pair to enclose

1. an internal series
2. abrupt changes in thought or pronounced sentence interrupters
3. parenthetical elements, often for emphasis
4. interrupting modifiers and appositives for dramatic effect

PARENTHESES:

1. to enclose words, phrases, or expressions that have no bearing upon the main idea (to make asides or "whispers" to the reader)

   NOTE: Like commas and dashes, parentheses may occasionally be used also:

2. to enclose an interrupting series
3. to enclose an appositive
4. to enclose an interrupting modifier between subject—verb

PERIOD:

1. at the end of a declarative sentence
2. after abbreviations

QUESTION MARK:

1. at the end of a direct question
2. after each question in a series
   Where are the jewels? the crown? the rings? the tiaras?
3. in parentheses to express uncertainty
   In 1340 (?) Chaucer was born.

   NOTE: Don't use a question mark to indicate

   a. *intended irony:* His humorous letter failed to amuse her.

b. *an indirect question:* Joe asked when we were going to have chiles rellenos again.

c. *courteous requests:* Will you please pass the butter.

EXCLAMATION POINT:

1. at the end of sentences with strong exclamations or commands, those that show strong emotion
2. after strong interjections

QUOTATION MARKS:

1. ALWAYS AFTER periods and commas
2. ALWAYS BEFORE colons and semicolons
3. before or after question marks and exclamation points, depending upon the context of the sentence
4. to enclose the actual words of a speaker
5. to identify symbols, letters, words used as such (He has too many "but's" in this paragraph, and his "$" sign is a simple "S.")
6. to enclose the titles of short stories, short poems, paintings, songs, magazine articles, essays, chapters of books, BUT NOT book titles

BRACKETS:

1. to enclose words of the writer, such as different verb tenses, or to alter punctuation in the original quoted material
2. to alert the reader to an error in quoted material

   NOTE: Use brackets around the Latin term *sic* to indicate the error in the quoted passage, such as an incorrect name, date, or spelling. [*sic*]

Suggested Review Questions

PATTERN NUMBERS	
1 and 3	**1.** Explain the difference between a compound sentence with a semicolon and one with a colon. What is the specific difference in the second clause?
2	**2.** What kind of verb must be "understood" in the second clause before you can omit it? Can you ever omit something other than the verb in an elliptical construction?
4–8	**3.** What kinds of things can be listed in series? What slots in the sentence can contain series? Explain the patterns and the punctuation for the different kinds of series.
	4. In PATTERN 6, what two things come immediately after the series of appositives?
	5. Why must the series in PATTERN 7 be set off by a pair of dashes? What other marks of punctuation might occasionally substitute for those dashes?
	6. In what two particular places in an essay would PATTERN 8 be good to use? What should go into the dependent clause?
	7. What other patterns can perform the same function?
9	**8.** What qualifications should a word have before you put it in PATTERN 9?
9a	**9.** What kinds of words and in what slots of the sentence can you repeat the same word in parallel structure?
9	**10.** What kind of construction must come after the comma to keep PATTERN 9 from becoming a PATTERN 1 with a comma splice?
	11. Write one sentence three times, using different

PATTERN NUMBERS	
10 and 10a	punctuation marks before the appositive (comma, dash, colon). Then explain the difference in emphasis that the punctuation creates. Which is least emphatic? Which is most emphatic? Which makes a longer pause? Which is most formal and prim?
	12. What besides a single word can be an appositive?
	13. *a.* What is the difference between the construction following the colon in PATTERN 3 and the one following the colon in PATTERN 10?
	b. What is the difference between the construction following the dash in PATTERN 9 and the one following the dash in PATTERN 10a?
7a and 11	**14.** Explain the difference between an internal appositive and an interrupting modifier.
11	**15.** In PATTERN 11, what two main parts of the sentence are separated by this interrupting modifier?
11	**16.** What three marks of punctuation can separate this modifier from the rest of the sentence? Can you ever use just ONE of these marks?
	17. Write the same sentence three times. Punctuate it with a pair of commas, a pair of dashes, and a pair of parentheses; then explain the difference in sound and emphasis in each.
11a	**18.** Write a sentence that functions as an interrupting modifier in another sentence.
11a	**19.** Write a question as an interrupting modifier. Where does the question mark go?
12	**20.** Where do participles come from? How are they

PATTERN NUMBERS		
		always used? What different kinds of endings may they have?
12	**21.**	How can you avoid a dangling participle here?
13	**22.**	What kind of modifier needs a comma after it in PATTERN 13?
14	**23.**	What does "inverted sentence" mean?
15	**24.**	What purpose might lead you to invert a sentence?
15	**25.**	What items in the normal order of a sentence may come out of their normal place (i.e., be inverted)?
15a	**26.**	What cautions must you observe to make your inversions successful?
16	**27.**	What kind of phrases (words) always come in pairs?
16	**28.**	What kind of statement will this pattern help you to make?
17	**29.**	What kind of "signal words" begin dependent clauses that may function as subject or object or complement?
	30.	Write two sentences using the same dependent clause. In one sentence, make the dependent clause the subject; in another, make it the direct object.
18	**31.**	Describe an absolute construction; name its two parts. Can it ever be a complete sentence?
18	**32.**	What is the difference in this pattern and the one with an introductory or concluding modifier?

PATTERN NUMBERS	
18	**33.** If the absolute construction occurs in the middle of the sentence, what must your punctuation be?
18	**34.** Can absolute constructions ever occur in pairs or in series?
19	**35.** What is the difference between PATTERN 19 and the ordinary kind of short simple sentence?
19	**36.** What special functions can this pattern perform?
19	**37.** Why is the sound of this pattern so important? the rhythm? the context?
19a	**38.** What special functions can the short question perform?
19a	**39.** What are the two types of questions?
19a	**40.** Where are good places to use a short question in writing?
20	**41.** What two reasons may make a writer use a deliberate fragment?
20	**42.** What is the importance of the surrounding context for a deliberate fragment?
20	**43.** What different kinds of functions may the fragment perform?

MISCELLANEOUS QUESTIONS (for class discussion or essay tests)

44. Write the same sentence twice and punctuate it two different ways. Discuss the difference in sound, emphasis, and effect.

45. Write a sentence with S–V–D.O. Now put the D.O. in a different place and notice the effect.

46. Express the same idea with different kinds of phrasing:

Bad grades bother John.
What bothers John is bad grades.
John is bothered by bad grades.
John, bothered by bad grades, decided to burn some midnight oil.
Bad grades bothering John?
Bad grades having bothered him before, John determined that this semester would be different.

47. Make up some sentences with nonsense words and discuss the structure and punctuation involved.

48. Define certain terms that occur in CHAPTER 2: *elliptical, appositive, parallel, construction, participle, absolute construction, series, modifier.*

49. What function does punctuation play in most sentences?

50. Why are style and variety in your sentence structure so important anyway?

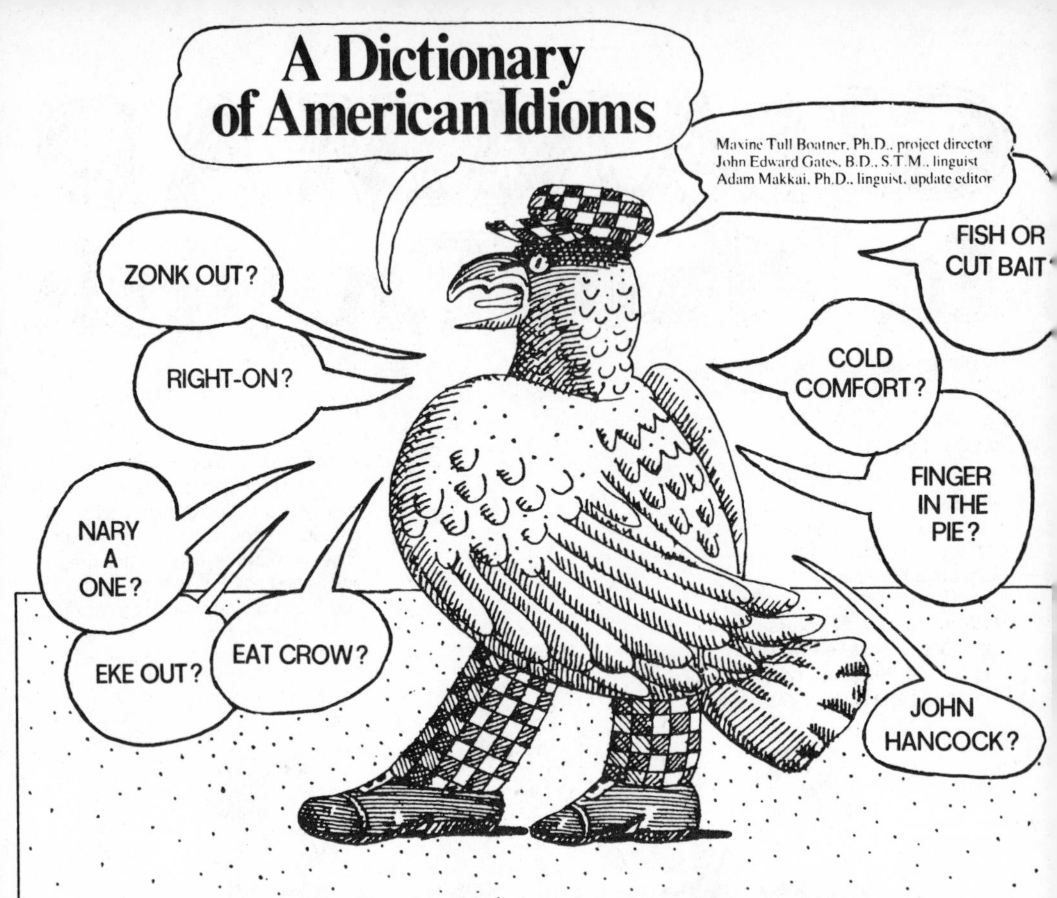

Idioms used in American English may be the richest in the world. They depict every possible mood and idea, and are derived from proverbs, events, and every imaginable source. As new ideas originate, new expressions appear to express them; that's how idioms are born. Idioms are *pre-existing* words, sometimes put together in combinations, which make *new* sense.

A Dictionary of American Idioms, published by Barron's Educational Series, Inc., is geared to a wide variety of people. By improving communication, this book will help bridge the gap between parents and kids. It is especially helpful for teachers who need to understand students better, for students with underdeveloped vocabularies, and for writers who want to be on top of new terms and expressions. This dictionary is also vital for ethnic groups and nonnative English speakers who want to make their command of American English more fluent. It is totally up-to-date.

To further enhance the study value of the *Dictionary of American Idioms,* the labels *slang, formal, literary, vulgar, substandard, nonstandard, cliche, archaic, British,* and *Southern* are attached to delineate each idiom. The book thus indicates when it is suitable to use the expressions—and, just as importantly, when *not* to use them. The dictionary features an appendix of essential idioms. $9.95 pa.

"The selection of entries (4,000), the clear definitions, and the helpful, natural examples in *A Dictionary of American Idioms* will provide English speakers—native and non-native—with an invaluable guide to what Americans are really saying when they talk."

Laurence Urdang, Editor
Verbatim

All prices are in U.S. dollars and subject to change without notice. At your local bookseller, or order direct adding 15% postage (minimum charge $1.50) plus applicable sales tax.

BARRON'S

113 Crossways Park Drive, Woodbury, New York 11797

10 Steps in Writing the Research Paper
Markman and Waddell 160 pp., $4.95
The process of writing a research paper is reduced to 10 simple steps. Plus a unique section on "Plagiarism: A Step to Avoid."

The Art of Styling Sentences: 20 Patterns to Success
Wadell, Esch, and Walker
112 pp., $4.95
By imitating 20 sentence patterns and variations, students will grasp how to write with imagination, clarity, and style. Illustrated with practice material for writing more effectively.

Spelling Your Way to Success
Mersand and Griffith 224 pp., $5.95
A systematic, simplified, and progressive method of improving one's spelling without constantly having to consult a dictionary. Numerous self-tests and practice material.

Building an Effective Vocabulary
Cedric Gale 288 pp., $5.50
A thorough course in all the methods of evaluating words for richness and appropriateness to improve ability to communicate.

1001 Pitfalls in English Grammar
Vincent F. Hopper 352 pp., $5.95
The most common errors in the English language are examined, including grammar, spelling, word choice, and punctuation.

1100 Words You Need to Know
Bromberg and Gordon 220 pp., $5.95
More than 1100 words and idioms taken from the mass media and introduced in readable stories. Contains 46 daily lessons of 20 minutes each.

Essentials of English
Hopper, Foote, Gale 256 pp., $5.50
A comprehensive program in the writing skills necessary for effective communication.

Essentials of Writing
Hopper and Gale 176 pp., $5.95
A companion workbook for the material in ESSENTIALS OF ENGLISH.

Word Mastery: A Guide to the Understanding of Words
Drabkin, Bromberg 224 pp., $6.95
This fascinating book stresses word use and word development through the presentation of words in natural settings such as newspapers and magazines. With practice exercises.

How to Write Themes and Term Papers
Barbara Lenmark Ellis 160 pp., $5.50
The correct, logical approach to tackling a theme project or paper.

Words with a Flair
Bromberg and Liebb 224 pp., $6.95
A collection of 600 difficult but useful words. Includes word games and puzzles.

Getting Your Words Across
Murray Bromberg and Milton Katz
224 pp., $5.95
A unique new basic vocabulary book utilizing brief articles, exercises and crossword puzzles to help build word power.

A Pocket Guide to Correct Punctuation
Robert Brittain 96 pp., $2.95
Explains what each mark means, and shows how to use it with clarity and precision.

A Pocket Guide to Correct English
Michael Temple 128 pp., $2.95
A concise guide to the essentials of correct grammar and usage, spelling, punctuation, writing, and more.

A Pocket Guide to Correct Spelling
Francis Griffith 256 pp., $2.95
A handy quick-reference tool that lists 25,000 words in alphabetical order, correctly spelled and divided into syllables.

Barron's "Easy Way" Series: English Titles
Three practical guides filled with straightforward instruction and numerous examples.

English the Easy Way
Harriet Diamond and Phyllis Dutwin
224 pp., $7.95

Spelling the Easy Way
Joseph Mersand and Francis Griffith
144 pp., $7.95

Typing the Easy Way
Warren T. Schimmel and
Stanley A. Lieberman
144 pp., $8.95

Handbook of Commonly Used Idioms
Maxine Tull Boatner and
Jonathan Edward Gates
Update Editor Adam Makkai
224 pp., $5.95
A fascinating and useful book for people learning English as well as for "natives" who want to add color and variety to their conversations. Includes 1500 popular idioms.

How to Beat Test Anxiety and Score Higher on Your Exams
James H. Divine and David W. Kylen
144 pp., $3.50
This reassuring book will help nervous test-takers of all ages gain skill and confidence. The authors reveal how test-taking skills can be learned; how basic preparation techniques can reduce anxiety and improve performance.
"Excellent book!" — J. Wiseman, Student Education Center, Philadelphia, Pa.

Study Tactics
William H. Armstrong 272 pp., $5.50
For students who want to earn higher grades, this useful guide presents an easy-to-follow plan for sound study habits. Pointers on mastering writing techniques, increasing reading speed reviewing for exams, and more are given.

Barron's Better Grades in College With Less Effort
Kenneth A. Green 176 pp., $4.95
How to cope with college work is analyzed in this survival kit. Includes legitimate shortcuts to better grades with minimal hassles.

You Can Succeed! The Ultimate Study Guide for Students
Eric Jensen 208 pp., $3.95
This positive guide to success in school encourages high school students to make a contract with themselves to set goals and work ambitiously toward them. Among the topics covered: Lack of Motivation—the #1 Problem, Success Habits, Attack Plan for Studying, Using Your Memory More Effectively, Word Power, How to Take Tests.

Study Tips How to Study Effectively and Get Better Grades
William H. Armstrong 272 pp., $3.95
A guide to improving the skills necessary to earn higher grades in many subjects at many levels. Tips on how to master writing techniques, improve study habits, increase reading speed, review for exams, and more.

How to Find What You Want in the Library
Charlotte Gorden 144 pp., $5.95
A handy and educational guide to library use. Written in an appealing style, it teaches high school students how to use a card catalog, locate books, and do research for term papers.